THE GOD CONCLUSION

SARUM THEOLOGICAL LECTURES

THE GOD CONCLUSION

*God and the Western
Philosophical Tradition*

Keith Ward

DARTON·LONGMAN + TODD

First published in 2009 by
Darton, Longman and Todd Ltd
1 Spencer Court
140–142 Wandsworth High Street
London SW18 4JJ

ISBN 978-0-232-52757-1

A catalogue record is available for this book from the British Library.

Phototypeset by YHT Ltd, London
Printed and bound in Great Britain by Athenaeum Press Ltd, Gateshead,
Tyne & Wear

CONTENTS

INTRODUCTION

This book defends one main thesis. It is that the Western classical tradition in philosophy – found in the works of the 'great philosophers' who would normally be studied in Colleges – accepts the God conclusion. There is a supreme spiritual (non-physical) reality which is the cause or underlying nature of the physical cosmos, and which is of great, and maybe the greatest possible, value or perfection.

The book is a defence of this thesis, because the thesis has in recent years been denied, dismissed, or simply overlooked by many writers. It is important to remember our intellectual history, and to remember that belief in God has usually been expounded by the best-known philosophers as the most rational view of the world. Such belief has hardly ever been regarded as a matter of 'blind faith' or of some irrational leap in the dark. It lies at the very basis of acceptance of the intelligibility of the universe, of the importance of morality, and of a deep understanding of the nature of human existence.

In defending this thesis, I have also taken the opportunity to defend many 'lost causes', to try to correct some widely held but mistaken ideas about what philosophers have believed, and to defend a few currently unfashionable ideas. So I hope my defence will be entertainingly provocative as well as being correct.

Thus I defend Plato against Sir Karl Popper's attack on him as an enemy of the 'open society'. I defend Aquinas' 'Five Ways' of demonstrating the existence of God. I show that Descartes was not what is usually described as a 'Cartesian dualist'. I defend (to a great extent) Bishop Berkeley's immaterialism. I attack with some vigour David Hume's arguments against God. I show that

Kant did not destroy all possible arguments for God. I try to show that Hegel is not unintelligible, that Schopenhauer was not really an atheist, and that Nietzsche got into an irretrievable mess about freedom. I conclude by arguing that modern materialism is probably already out of date, and that at the very least it is an incomplete theory on a number of counts. If accepted it would of course rule out the existence of God. But I argue that it is not a strong enough theory to bring the main Western theistic tradition to an end.

The book is not really about the philosophy of religion. It is about philosophy insofar as its major concerns impinge upon religion. The connections are quite close, since some major philosophical questions are concerned with the ultimate nature of reality, the nature of the human person, questions of meaning, value and purpose, and questions of responsibility, freedom and morality.

Philosophers have something of a reputation for independence of mind and scepticism, and they usually dislike being thought of as defenders of any sort of orthodoxy. There are some notable defenders of orthodox belief, like Thomas Aquinas. But even he was banned from teaching for a while by the Bishop of Paris, and his views were thought to be very advanced in the thirteenth century.

Nevertheless it is the case that most major philosophers have inclined to a roughly Idealist view of the world – they have thought that there is something mind-like at the basis of things, or that values are in some sense objective. There has always been an anti-Idealist opposition, and it still exists today. Some of the best-known philosophers of recent times have inclined to reductionist or materialist views of one sort or another, though they are in fact a minority among professional philosophers.

I intend to treat matters historically, moving from the ancient Greeks, by way of late medieval Christendom and the Enlightenment, to recent emphasis on problems of consciousness and artificial intelligence. It may seem an unduly European or 'Western' history. But it is in Europe that philosophy, understood as the pursuit of critical and independent thinking, has flourished. It may only be part of a rich and much more varied global heritage of thought. But the problems it has dealt with, and the way in which it has dealt with them, remain characteristic of a specific tradition of thought that was born in Greece and flourished conspicuously in Europe after the Enlightenment. So it may be seen as one important tradition of human thought.

Some might hold that the tradition has now come to an end. But I think that, on the contrary, it still has a great deal of importance to contribute to human understanding of the world. I think it is vital to consider the questions about God it raises in a serious, critical and informed way, and not to let discussions about God degenerate, as these days they often do, into a conflict of unsubstantiated prejudices. I also think that philosophy, while it is serious, should also be fun. I hope it is.

Chapter 1

WHY PLATO WAS NOT A WORLD-HATING TOTALITARIAN

All agree that philosophy really begins, as far as a substantial set of writings is concerned, with Plato. He clearly formulated the two fundamental questions of philosophy: 'What do you mean?' and 'How do you know?' In his Dialogues he gets his hero, usually Socrates, to demonstrate to others that they do not really know exactly what they mean by most of the terms they use. And Socrates' victims are usually unable to explain how they know the things they claim to know. Perhaps the historical Socrates, who was condemned by the Athenian democracy for impiety and for corrupting the youth, had just annoyed too many people too much. And so philosophers continue to annoy today.

Plato, of course, was not Socrates. Plato was an aristocrat who wrote books, while Socrates was not. Plato, especially later in his life, developed some quite positive and dogmatic views, which probably did not originate with Socrates. And Plato made a rather feeble and unsuccessful attempt to construct a political system in Crete, and to draw up plans for a perfect state which are of quite Draconian strictness.

Partly for that reason, Plato has been demonised by some as a reactionary and repressive autocrat. Karl Popper's book, *The Open Society and Its Enemies*,[1] depicts Plato as one of the great enemies of liberal democracy. And it is true that Plato presented democracy as the second worst of all political systems in his dialogue *The Republic*.[2] He depicts the perfect society as an aristocracy, but it is more like what we might call a meritocracy, government by the wise, by an aristocracy of the mind.

But Plato suggests that, even if such a society ever actually could exist, it would inevitably decline by successively worse stages. First would come timocracy, where the love of honour and military might, of pride and ambition, would predominate. Plato is here thinking of Athens' great enemy, Sparta, which had just won a war against Athens, and was a strongly disciplined militaristic society, ruling over a class of virtual slaves.

This would in turn decline into plutocracy, the rule of the rich. After that would come democracy, which Plato characterises as 'the rule of the mob'. And finally would come the worst of all states, despotism, the rule of a dictator, when reason and justice have been almost wholly eradicated, and the will of the tyrant is the only law.

This is a rather gloomy prognosis, and it is interesting to see how Karl Marx used a very similar progression for his analysis of human history, though he gave it what was meant to be a much more positive interpretation. For Marx, aristocratic reason had never ruled. But the feudal system was, for him, a form of timocracy; capitalism succeeded it, and was in effect the rule of the rich. Democracy was the rule of the bourgeoisie, and was to be succeeded by the dictatorship of the proletariat. Whereas for Plato this succession was a decline, for Marx it was a historically inevitable and progressive liberation from ancient tyranny. It would all end, as Plato's had begun, with a perfect society. But for Marx the Communist society would be one in which all are equal and all take just what they need, and give to society what they are able.

Popper was in a sense correct in seeing both Plato and Marx as historicists, seeing inevitable processes at work in history. But their attitudes to those processes were quite different. Plato, out of fear of them, adopted an attitude calculated to prevent any change. Marx, out of approval of them, called for constant revolution to overthrow the old and help bring in the new.

There is another major difference, too. Marx was primarily a political theorist and activist, whose purpose was to change the structures of society. The lives of individuals would change in

---

consequence, he thought. Plato, on the other hand, ends Book 9 of *The Republic* by conceding that the perfect society probably exists nowhere on earth. But, he says, 'Perhaps there is a pattern set up in the heavens for one who desires to see it, and, seeing it, to found one in himself. But whether it exists anywhere or will exist is no matter; for this is the only commonwealth in whose politics he can ever take part.'[3]

These words were to be influential on both Stoics and Christians. Christians can hardly fail, reading them, to think of Jesus' words, 'Thy kingdom come on earth as it is in heaven.' The pattern of the rule of the Good, perfectly instantiated in the intelligible world, can, at least to some extent, take form in human souls. And Plato hints, or more than hints, throughout *The Republic*, that the soul that is patterned on the commonwealth of the Good (verbally paralleled in the Christian New Testament by talk of 'the kingdom of God') will find itself a stranger and a pilgrim on the earth, mocked by those still chained in and deluded by the shadows of the cave.

Plato's interest is quite different from that of Marx. Plato is concerned with the rule of justice in the hearts of men and women, with their ascent to the vision of the Good, and with their escape from the cave of ignorance. Marx regarded all that as a betrayal of the human responsibility to change society, and to stop the introspective heart-searching which would inevitably lead, he thought, to political apathy, and to the loss of any grip on reality.

And it is at just this point that Popper is not wholly fair to Plato. For Plato was not primarily a political reactionary who used his philosophy as a support for his political views. Nor is there any intrinsic connection between Plato's metaphysics and his politics. Indeed, his metaphysics can be used equally plausibly to support a much more libertarian and reformist political agenda.

It has to be accepted that Plato's own political views were non-libertarian. In *The Laws* he sketched the nature of the ideal state in greater detail, and the picture he drew must strike most

Why Plato Was Not a World-hating Totalitarian

moderns as wholly repressive. His imagined state, Magnesia, is to be forcibly locked into resistance to all change. It is, after all, perfect, so all change would be for the worse. No young person under forty is allowed to travel abroad for any reason. Even after that age, they cannot travel for purely private reasons or just for pleasure. Moreover, since moral standards are absolute and unchangeable, and can be known with certainty, such standards must be taught and enforced without permitting dissent. This extends as far as requiring the death penalty for anyone who establishes a shrine on private land, or who sacrifices on public land to 'gods not included in the pantheon of the state'.[4] No moral or religious reforms can ever be countenanced, since everything is just perfect as it is. This is a rather ironic conclusion for an admirer of Socrates, who was condemned for impiety towards the established Athenian gods.

Plato would be proud to plead guilty to the charge that his ideal society is both rigidly conservative (not countenancing change) and repressive of dissent. It is fairly easy to find the root principle that gives rise to his views, as it gives rise to many illiberal views. It is that there exists one absolute truth; that it can be known with certainty, probably by a small minority; that knowledge of it will entail virtuous living (following the Socratic principle that 'virtue is knowledge', so that no one who really knows what is right could ever do wrong); and that its principles can be successfully imposed by force, dissent being a form of culpable and dangerous ignorance.

This principle seems very widespread in human societies, whether they are religiously based or not. It is the principle, 'I know what is right, and I will brook no denial of it.' It is the complete opposite of the principle, 'It is very difficult to know what is right, and maybe I should listen to differing views to help me come to some decision, however provisional it may be.' But suppose we ask, which of these principles is really that of Plato?

The paradox is that he sometimes implies (in *The Laws*, for instance – in which, notably, Socrates does not appear) that he supports the first principle. But the form and content of his

Dialogues, taken as a whole, is a very strong expression of the second principle. The Dialogues of Plato are the first major written expression of critical thought and free enquiry in human history. And, being Dialogues, they do not all express one consistently upheld viewpoint – even the famous Theory of Forms is virtually refuted in the *Parmenides*. They are arguments, conversations, and they by no means end with clear statements of absolute truth. In every case, we end with the feeling that there is more to be said, and that, when we have recovered from the long night's drinking, the discussions will continue. More than that, it is the process of argumentation, of enquiry and reflection, which is of value, not just the presentation of a dogma.

We might try to explain this by saying that Plato was an aristocratic dogmatist trying to express the thoughts of a social gadfly (Socrates, a disturber of received opinions). That is probably true. But another suggestion is that even his most dogmatic statements may in truth be the statements of a gadfly, meant to spur us on to further reflection – as they have done for over two millennia. Perhaps his depiction of Magnesia, the perfect society, is ironic, the picture of an impossibility. It is the picture of a society of perfected individuals, for whom punishment is no longer needed, who gladly assent to the rule of the wise, who are also incorruptible.

What would be foolish would be to try to build such a society out of weak and corruptible human beings. As Plato said in the dialogue *Meno*, virtue can neither be taught, nor is it natural. It is, where it exists, 'a divine dispensation'.[5] It is a gift of the gods. Though genuine knowledge of the Good may engender virtue, because evil becomes unthinkable for one who truly knows the Good, such knowledge is rare, and is liable to be mocked by most humans, imprisoned as they are in the cave of ignorance.

Indeed, insofar as Plato really is a historicist, he is bound to think that a perfect society cannot resist change and degeneration, however much the ruling class tries to prevent it. So, as Karl Popper says, it is more important, in building a human society, to seek the best means of avoiding tyranny rather than to try to

Why Plato Was Not a World-hating Totalitarian

establish an unchanging Utopia. Out of the crooked timber of humanity, as Immanuel Kant was to say, nothing perfect can be built. Plato should have realised this more clearly; but the truth is that politics was not his strong suit, or his primary concern.

What Plato places before us, especially in *The Republic*, is a picture of human life in which the passions and desires are ruled by Reason, and Reason is ruled by knowledge of that which is absolutely and flawlessly good. This knowledge is described by Socrates' great speech in the *Symposium*, which I cannot resist quoting at length:

> The man who has been guided thus far in the mysteries of love, and who has directed his thoughts towards examples of beauty in due and orderly succession, will suddenly have revealed to him as he approaches the end of his initiation a beauty whose nature is marvellous indeed, the final goal of all his previous efforts. This beauty is first of all eternal; it neither comes into being nor passes away, neither waxes nor wanes; next, it is not beautiful in part and ugly in part, nor beautiful at one time and ugly at another, nor beautiful in this relation and ugly in that, nor beautiful here and ugly there, as varying according to its beholders; nor again will this beauty appear to him like the beauty of a face or hands or anything else corporeal, or like the beauty of a thought or a science, or like the beauty which has its seat in something other than itself, be it a living thing or the earth or the sky or anything else whatever; he will see it as absolute, existing alone with itself, unique, eternal, and all other beautiful things as partaking of it, yet in such a manner that, while they come into being and pass away, it neither undergoes any increase or diminution nor suffers any change ... a man's life should be spent in the contemplation of absolute beauty ... and he will be able to bring forth not mere reflected images of goodness but true goodness, because he will be in contact not with a reflection but with the truth. And having brought forth and nurtured true goodness he will have the

privilege of being beloved of God, and becoming, if ever a man can, immortal himself.[6]

Whether or not Socrates ever said such a thing as this, it is the foundation of much of Augustine's thought and of the tradition of neo-Platonism which flourished in Alexandria, where early Christian theology most fruitfully developed. Plato makes Socrates ascribe this teaching to a woman, Diotima, and Socrates does not claim to have achieved such knowledge himself. Thus again there is a stress on the difficulty and rarity of such absolute knowledge, which makes it very unlikely that it could be institutionalised in any social class, like the Philosopher-Kings of the Republic. Political thought for the shadow-world in which we live calls for much more compromise and adjustment than Plato gave it. But to make such adjustments is in fact called for by Plato's deepest philosophical stance, which places the Republic of the Good in the realm of the eternal, and always beyond this transient world, which can only ever partly and dimly partake of it.

The doctrine of the 'participation' of the temporal in the eternal is one that also places in question a common view of Plato as a hater of the world and of material bodies. It is true that he in one place calls the body the 'tomb' of the soul, and that he looks for the final destiny of all souls far beyond this embodied world. He is, in a sense that Descartes never was, a fully-fledged dualist. Yet in the *Timaeus* – the only text of Plato generally known in Europe in the early Middle Ages – he describes time as 'the moving image of eternity'.[7] And he holds that the created universe is so perfect that it is indeed 'a blessed god'.[8]

These are not the words of a world-hater. The world is the finite image of eternal beauty. Again Christians must be reminded of a statement of Paul, or of a follower of his, about the person of Jesus Christ: 'he is the visible image of the invisible God' (Col. 1:15). If there ever was a being that could be a clear image of eternity, then it would be united in being to the Eternal, and would mediate its beauty and goodness to the world. It would be the image and the mediator of the Good in the

Why Plato Was Not a World-hating Totalitarian

darkness of the cave – though, Plato remarks, such a being would probably be mocked and killed by those who take darkness rather than light to be the ultimate reality.

Plato's overall view expresses a dialectic between two extremes – one that the world is evil and to be escaped from, and the other that the world is a 'blessed god', a perfect finite image of divine Beauty. There is actually no 'final system' in Plato's works. The Dialogues present differing viewpoints – even the much-maligned Sophists of ancient Greece are accorded a mixture of respect and contempt, in the *Protagoras*, for example. It was left to later thinkers, like Plotinus, to systematise some of the central themes of Plato's works, and to connect them to a religious, or at least a mystical, way of life.

Plato's remarks about a supreme reality include references to a personal Demiurge, or Intelligent Designer of the universe; a more impersonal principle of the Good and Beautiful, which is 'beyond even being'; and a world of Forms or Ideas, which is the archetype for every material being. The third-century thinker Plotinus (AD 204–70), or his teacher Ammonius Saccas, systematised many of these remarks, and devised the idea of a Divine Triad – the One, beyond all conceptual thought; the Logos, or intellectual principle, in which all the essential natures of things, all possible states of affairs and ideals, exist; and the World-Soul, which gives actuality and life to particular entities that comprise the universe.

The One generates from itself, without being changed or diminished, the Logos, which in turn generates the World-Soul. From that divine Triad, the whole finite universe flows by necessity. At each level beings both continue to generate fainter, more remote images of the Divine Triad, and also strive to reflect more perfectly their divine source. Every possible degree of being is generated, until at last being runs out into its last and most imperfect forms, the forms of darkness we call, by contrast with higher modes of being, 'evil'. Within this world, human souls, fallen into an alien material realm, strive to return to the One source, in what Plotinus calls 'the flight of the alone to the

Alone',[9] the return of the separated soul to the completed fullness of that which needs no companion.

One of Plotinus' fellow-pupils was, it is reported, the Christian theologian Origen, and the Christian doctrine of God as Trinity is clearly influenced by this form of Platonism. Throughout the Bible there is talk of the Spirit of God 'hovering over' creation, of the Wisdom of God delighting in the created world, and of the transcendence of God, of which no image can be made. In the New Testament Jesus is identified by John with the Wisdom or Logos, and the Spirit that overshadowed the disciples at Pentecost was formally defined as divine by the first Council of Constantinople in AD 381. Platonism provided the concepts in terms of which Christian orthodoxy was defined, and enshrined the Trinitarian nature of God at the heart of the new religion.

There are of course also marked differences between this neo-Platonism and what became Christian orthodoxy. It is more a matter of influence than of straightforward borrowing. For example, Plotinus' One is beyond consciousness and intention. The Logos flows from it without conscious desire or intention, as does everything else, and it might have been better, Plotinus remarks, for the universe not to exist – it just necessarily does exist. There is not one Father of all who consciously and freely wills to create a universe, when there were other possibilities available.

Again, for Christians, souls do not seek to return by their own ascetic efforts to an undifferentiated unity in which any sense of individual separateness or social relationship is lost. Plotinus regarded the idea of the resurrection of the body as a barbaric superstition, and the idea of a Saviour as just a refusal to take responsibility for your own fate.

Yet the basic Platonic idea that the whole sensory and material world is the appearance of an underlying spiritual reality, which is rational and intelligible, and which ultimately flows from a being of supreme beauty and goodness – that idea became central to Christian orthodoxy. And, despite the misgivings of Plotinus and of the later Platonist Porphyry, who also opposed Christianity, the basic Christian belief in a God who creates the universe intentionally as an overflowing of the divine goodness and beauty, and who is incarnate in the world in a finite image of the world's eternal archetype, is a natural development of some major strands of Platonism.

Belief in one God who creates this universe for the sake of the beauty and value that can only exist within it, and belief that the cosmos is an image of eternal beauty and wisdom, can be found in Plato, especially in the *Timaeus*. Even belief that God becomes incarnate is deeply consonant with Plato's doctrine that a good being will seek to help those who suffer, and that finite things can be greater or lesser images of the infinite God. We might think, then, that a supremely good God might seek to help humans who are (as Plotinus says) lost in ignorance and darkness, and might do so by providing a finite image of the divine in a perfected human life. We might also think that a good God would seek to share its goodness in conscious relationship to finite persons, who might find the fulfilment of their personal and social lives in God. This thought, however, probably pushes the idea of activity, relationship, and change in God further than Plato was prepared to go.

It is not quite right to say that Christianity is just a series of footnotes to Plato. But Plato lived four centuries before Jesus. Greek temples have been discovered in Galilee, and some mystical strands of Jewish thought, and maybe quite a lot of John's Gospel, undoubtedly show Greek influence. Perhaps the teaching of Jesus himself about the Kingdom of God, although phrased in terms of the mythology of Jewish apocalyptic thought, embodied the secret teaching that the Kingdom is the rule of perfect Beauty, inscribed by divine dispensation in the hearts of men and women who hunger and thirst for true goodness. Perhaps Plato was, at least to some extent, as Augustine said, 'a Christian before Christ'. Or we could put that in another way, and say – though admittedly it would not be the whole truth – that Christianity is Platonism personalised.

Chapter 2

WHY AQUINAS' 'FIVE WAYS' ARE NOT SO BAD AFTER ALL

The pupil and successor of Plato in Athens was Aristotle (384–322 BC), who founded his own philosophical school, the Lyceum. The philosophy of Aristotle dominated the later medieval period in Europe, and was influential on both Islam and Christianity.

Generally speaking, philosophy in the Middle Ages was very much the handmaid of theology. This is so to such an extent that when I took my philosophy degree, no philosopher was mentioned who lived in medieval times, and the history of philosophy went straight from Aristotle to Descartes.

This was a very misleading view of the history of ideas, and depends upon a much more recent opinion that philosophy and theology are wholly distinct from and even opposed to one another. The reason for this is, I suppose, that theology is seen as a confessional discipline. It defends the beliefs of a Church or religious organisation, and so is primarily apologetic. Philosophy, however, is by nature critical of all creeds and organisations, and it may issue arguments in defence of atheism as well as in defence of religious views.

That view may now be held quite widely, but it is not the only possible view, and it is not the one I myself hold. Theology may also be seen as the systematic intellectual study of beliefs and practices concerning *theos*, God. These beliefs need not be those of any specific religious organisation. There are Christian theologies, Muslim theologies, Jewish and Hindu theologies. It may seem that Buddhists have been left out, and it does feel odd to speak of Buddhist theology. Surprisingly, perhaps, some Buddhists do so, and that is because the word *theos* can be taken to refer to 'that which is taken to be ultimately real, or of supreme transcendent value'. Many Buddhists have beliefs about what is ultimately real – the flow of thoughts, feelings, and sensations that go to make up human experience, perhaps – and about what is of supreme transcendent value – Nirvana, a supra-human state of intelligence and bliss.

It may now seem that I am using theology to cover absolutely anything, but that is not so. There are philosophical investigations about the human person, language, the nature of knowledge, and many other topics, which do not directly speak of what, if anything, is ultimately real or of supreme transcendent value. That department of philosophy that deals with these latter questions is often called 'metaphysics', the study of what ultimate sorts of things and values there are.

Am I, then, equating theology and metaphysics? In a sense I am, and I am in very good company. Aristotle's *Metaphysics* (so called because it is the book of his collected works that comes after the book on physics) could equally well have been called his *Theology*. It certainly contains important discussions of God and of the ultimate natures of things. It is not, of course, Christian, but Christian theology is only one sub-branch of general theology.

In this sense an atheist could be a theologian, but most atheists I know would be appalled at the prospect. So it must be admitted that those who call themselves theologians usually are concerned with the exposition and analysis of the beliefs of one or more religious organisations, or of their holy texts. They need not agree with those beliefs, but the study of allegedly revealed beliefs is their primary concern.

It does not follow that theology, in this rather narrower sense, has to be apologetic. It need not be committed to defending the beliefs of one particular religious institution. Nor is it the case that all philosophers are critical of every sort of belief. Many philosophers are extremely dogmatic in their beliefs, and are not embarrassed to write apologetics in favour of such beliefs. So a philosopher may well hold religious beliefs, and write apologetics in favour of them.

That does not stop such writings beings properly philosophical. It is quite possible for a metaphysical philosopher to decide that there are good reasons for believing that there is a God. In that case it will be reasonable to think that God may have revealed the divine nature and purpose, and not just left it to humans to discover such things (which are probably hidden in the recesses of the divine mind) for themselves. If one such revelation is judged to be authentic, it will be reasonable to incorporate its content into a general metaphysical system.

The divine revelation will not contradict the metaphysics, presumably, but it may fulfil it and modify it in some respects. In that case, a metaphysician may turn into a systematic theologian, by incorporating into the metaphysical system some data obtained from revelation. The transition may be painless, and it could even be illuminating.

This exactly captures the position of philosophers like Thomas Aquinas, who took the philosophy of Aristotle and modified it in accordance with Christian revelation to form what they believed to be a more adequate philosophical view. It is very wide of the mark to suggest that Anselm and Aquinas were forced to toe some Catholic line, and just used philosophy to back up a set of acceptable beliefs. There is no reason to doubt that they found in the philosophy of Aristotle a compelling metaphysical system, which seemed to lead naturally to Christian belief in a creator God, whose revelation in Christ confirmed and amplified a generally Aristotelian metaphysics.

The turn from Plato to Aristotle that took place in the Western Church in the tenth and eleventh centuries is one that marks a difference in approach between the Eastern Orthodox Churches and the Roman Catholic Church. The Orthodox Churches place much emphasis on the ultimate mystery of the divine *ousia*, on icons as finite images of the infinite God, and on *theosis* – sharing in the divine nature – as the ultimate goal of human life.

So when it comes to the Holy Eucharist, for example, the Orthodox certainly believe that Christ is truly present in the bread and wine, but they usually prefer to think of this as a participation of human life in the divine life of supreme Goodness and Beauty, without going into too many details about the mechanics of the process. The Platonic approach is to accept the participation of the finite in the infinite, without detailing any specific conceptual definition of it.

The Catholic Church, however, at the Lateran Council of 1215, defined the doctrine of transubstantiation in Aristotelian terminology, holding that the accidents of bread and wine exist without an underlying substance, while they are the means of conveying the substance of Christ's body and blood to the believer. Both the use of Aristotelian terminology, and the concern to arrive at one correct and precise conceptual definition, are typical of the late medieval Catholic approach. We might say, with a measure of over-simplification, that the Orthodox Churches are Platonic, whereas the Catholic Church is Aristotelian.

Theologians like Aquinas make any claim that Christian faith is blind, unquestioning or irrational, absurd. If anything, the Thomist articulation of Christian faith is too rationalistic and too systematic to capture the diversity and mystery of Christian beliefs. What it is based upon is the postulate that the whole cosmos is the creation of a supremely intelligible and rational God, that humans, being made in the image of God, can follow the workings of the divine mind, at least to a great extent, and that the cosmos can be understood by the application of reason.

There are mysteries in the Christian faith, of course, though Aquinas gets them down to two – the Trinity and the Incarnation. Even then, it is easy to find rational arguments – in Richard of St Victor, for example – for why God should be exactly threefold, not more or less. And Anselm, in his great book *Cur Deus Homo?*, does not hesitate to provide reasons for why God had to become incarnate in order to redeem humans. He even calculates the exact number of humans who are going to be saved

– it turns out to be the number of fallen angels whose places in heaven now need to be filled.

Whether or not we now find such arguments compelling, there can be no doubt that they express a determination to find reasons for everything, to leave nothing irrational in God or in creation. In this way, late medieval Christian philosophy laid the foundation for the widespread modern scientific belief that the universe can be understood by human reason, and that it is an obligation to understand the cosmos, as a rational system, as fully as possible. Whatever that is, it is not a blind and non-rational faith.

Moreover, Aquinas was not a slave to a dogmatic and repressive Church. On the contrary, his works were among those condemned by the Bishop of Paris in 1277. Aristotle was considered by some to be a dangerously unorthodox, even possibly materialist, writer, whose views were incompatible with Christianity. It was not long, however, before Aquinas was to become the intellectual touch-stone of Catholic orthodoxy. All religion, like all human thought, contains anti-intellectual and repressive tendencies. But in Catholicism rationalism triumphed, and with it a strong belief in the capacity of human reason to work out or at least to provide the basis of fundamental beliefs about the nature of the cosmos and how humans should act in it.

The problem with taking Aristotle as the guide to a rational metaphysics and theology is that many of his beliefs about the natural world were wrong. He was wrong about the nature of the stars, the sun and moon, about inertia and the force of gravity, about the laws of motion and the atomic structure of matter. Moreover, some accuse him of being an impediment to the development of science for decades, if not for centuries. The seventeenth-century scientific writer Francis Bacon said that Aristotle's doctrine of final causes was 'like virgins dedicated to God, barren'. And it is arguable that modern science only really got under way when the search for the 'essential natures' of things, and for the final causes for the sake of which things exist, was given up.

Modern science is not concerned with essential natures, but

tends to see all material things as forming a continuum in which there are no sharp dividing class-divisions. And modern science is not concerned with whatever purposes nature might have, concerning itself solely with the general mathematically describable relationships that obtain between physical entities.

So on the one hand the rediscovery of Aristotle was a major factor in the rise of modern science. It encouraged investigation into the causes of things, to be discovered by close observation and the search for intellectual elegance. On the other hand, Aristotle's general view of nature as a realm in which Forms, or essential natures, were seeking to realise themselves ever more perfectly in matter because it is good that they should do so, stood in opposition to the modern scientific view of nature as a realm in which general laws of nature govern relations between objects, without any reference to purpose or value.

One way of resolving this paradox is to distinguish clearly between Aristotle's theories about physics and his metaphysical views. The Christian development of Aristotle's philosophy by Aquinas is of help here, because it frees natural science to investigate the laws in accordance with which physical entities behave, while holding that the purposes of nature are hidden in the mind of God. The natural sciences have no direct access to that mind, and some form of revelation may be necessary to give a clue as to what God's purposes are. Natural science will show the intelligibility and elegance of the laws of nature. But only philosophy can investigate the question of whether the whole of nature may be created for a purpose, and of whether there may be important aspects of the created order (like conscious thoughts and feelings, for instance) that cannot be fully investigated by the methods of the natural sciences.

Aristotle certainly did think there was a God, and he outlines his view of God in Book 12 of the *Metaphysics*. There he says:

> God is an eternal and most excellent living being, so that continuous and eternal life and duration belong to it ... it is without parts and indivisible, for it is moving things throughout

an infinite time ... it thinks of what is most divine and most valuable ... its life is like the best that we can enjoy ... and its contemplation is of all things the most pleasant ... it moves things by love. [This does not mean that it actively moves things, but that things change because of their attraction to it.][1]

This idea of God is not based on any revelation, and it is not an ordinary inductive causal inference from observation of what happens in the natural world. It is more like a fundamental postulate, the key integrating idea of a general conceptual scheme for interpreting the world in a consistent, coherent, plausible, fruitful and illuminating way.

Aristotle is thinking of God as an explanation for why the world is as it is. But he is thinking of a special kind of explanation, an explanation that will be final, in that it stands in need of no further explanation. An explanation is whatever answers the question 'Why?', and if you could think of something the very statement of which gives a wholly satisfactory answer to that question, so that it raised no further questions about why it is the way it is, then you would have a final explanation.

When Aquinas claims to set out five ways for demonstrating that God exists, at the beginning of the *Summa Theologiae*, he is expounding Aristotle's arguments in the *Metaphysics*.[2] The question both of them ask is: 'Is there any conceivable thing or state that could provide a final explanation for the existence and nature of the universe?'

Aquinas' first and second 'ways' point out that if anything changes or comes into being, such change or origination demands an explanation in terms of something other than the changed or originated thing. But then that 'something other' will need to be explained as well. So if it is to be something that does not need such a further explanation, it must be something different in kind from all changed or originated things. In other words, a finally satisfactory explanation of things that change or come-to-be would have to lie in something incapable of change or of coming into being.

Why Aquinas' 'Five Ways' Are Not So Bad After All

A timeless thing would fit the bill exactly. For if something is timeless, it is by definition incapable of change. And it cannot come into being, since then there would be a time when it was not, followed by a time at which it was – so it would be in time after all. There could, then, be a final explanation of things that change and come into being, and it would be some sort of timeless being or state. That is a fairly minimal definition, but at least it tells you something about what a final explanation would have to be. It would have to appeal to a being or state that is beyond time and change, that is eternal.

This form of argument does not appeal to everyone. Richard Dawkins, who has become a theologian or perhaps an anti-theologian in his old age, sees it as 'arbitrarily conjuring up a terminator' with an unwarranted assumption that God, the ter-minator, is immune to the regress.[3] But in fact to posit an unchangeable being or state as the explanation of a changing process is exactly what cosmologists do when they seek to explain the 'Big Bang'. They rightly sense that to just have an initial singularity at the origin of the universe is to leave it without final explanation. The search for explanation, which is the ultimate motivation of all science, would stop in a truly arbitrary state, which could not itself be explained.

So cosmologists search for something that could explain the Big Bang. And one favoured explanation at present is the pos-tulation of a set of unchanging quantum laws that govern a set of random quantum fluctuations in a vacuum. I am not here con-cerned to spell out what this means, and the difficulties of it, but the interesting point is that it is a proper scientific objective to find something that is not capable of being brought into being, and is not capable of change – such as a set of quantum laws that exist beyond all specific space-times, and that can explain how the universe originated as it did.

Dawkins remarks that it is 'perniciously misleading' to call this explanation God. But I think he has not got the patience to see what is going on, or how similar it is to proper scientific enquiry, admittedly at the edge of human understanding. What Aquinas is looking for is some final explanation for the universe. Following Aristotle, he claims that he can state some of the characteristics it must have. It must be beyond change and origination. It must be eternal.

But that is not yet sufficient for a truly final explanation. The as yet unanswered scientific question will be: why are those laws the way they are? And what Aquinas sees is that the only satisfactory answer to that question would be to show that there is simply no alternative. If you understand what the ultimate laws are, you will see that they have to be as they are; they could not be any other way. They are just necessary.

Does science come near that? It has made attempts. Steven Weinberg speaks of a 'final theory' as the only consistent mathematical formalism that could give rise to a universe containing intelligent life.[4] The laws are the way they are because if they were different, even very slightly, there would be no intelligent life. The laws are necessary to the universe being the way it is.

That is an amazing claim, that if the universe is the way it is, there is just one set of ultimate mathematical laws that could make it so. The claim is amazing because there is probably an infinite number of possible mathematical laws, and so the chance of this set existing is infinitely small. Nevertheless, the infinitely improbable might happen.

Yet even that is not quite good enough. For why should there be intelligent life? Why should there not be different laws that will not give rise to intelligent life? So mathematical physicists (some of them, anyway, and some of the very best of them) suppose that all possible mathematical formalisms exist. Mathematical truths, after all, are necessarily what they are – that is almost a definition of a mathematical truth. And if you had an exhaustive set of mathematical truths, that would be changeless and incapable of being brought into being or destroyed. The truths of mathematics are eternal and necessary. They are the nearest a mathematician gets to God.

At this point, the boundary between science and metaphysics

gets blurred. The existence of a Platonic mathematical realm, an exhaustive set of all mathematical truths, is not observationally verifiable or subject to experiment. It is a postulate that, for some mathematicians, underlies and justifies the basic axiom of scientific faith – that the cosmos is fully intelligible, and that it can be ultimately explained. In pursuit of this postulate, some cosmologists are today theorising that perhaps every mathematically possible universe does exist, generated by the necessary and eternal set of mathematical truths. We happen to exist in this universe, and perhaps, as Weinberg says, it is the only one in which intelligent life actually exists.

But where does God come into this? For Aquinas, as for Aristotle, God comes in because mathematical truths, while they are necessary and eternal, do not just exist on their own. Plato was mistaken if he thought they did. They exist, but not on their own. They exist, as all concepts do, in minds. And the complete and exhaustive set of all possible mathematical truths, as yet not by any means discovered by human mathematicians, exists in a cosmic mind, a cosmic consciousness whose thoughts they are.

God, on this account, is not the anthropomorphic bearded old man who finds parking-spaces for his favourite humans, as Dawkins seems to think he is. God is the cosmic mind whose content is the complete set of all mathematical truths. And once you have a cosmic mind, Aquinas clearly sees, you have a consciousness that can be aware of, evaluate, and discriminate between all the possibilities, mathematical and otherwise, that there are.

I sympathise with Richard Dawkins when he expresses a radical distaste for all these abstract and arcane considerations. It is the distaste zoologists might feel for cosmologists, or that practical scientists who dabble in test-tubes and rub up against real animals might feel for quantum physicists, who write their crazy thoughts on the backs of envelopes in arcane mathematical symbols. I sympathise; but I cannot agree that all this is mumbo-jumbo or anti-rational. Quite the contrary – this is the quest of reason pressed to its final limit.

Aquinas, though he lived long before the advent of modern cosmologists, is asking the questions they now ask. What could be a final explanation for the universe? Could it be a cosmic mind, that envisages all mathematically consistent possibilities, that evaluates intelligent life as good and as worth existing, and that for that very reason brings into being this finite world, perhaps the only finite world in which intelligent life can exist?

Aristotle closed the gap that existed in Plato between the world of Forms (all the mathematically possible states of affairs there could ever be) and the Demiurge that created the world on their pattern. Plato never quite managed to tie the Forms and the *Demiurgos* together in a plausible way.

For Aristotle, however, the Forms do not and cannot exist on their own. Forms only exist in things; but one of those things is the supreme cosmic mind, which patterns the world on them. How does such patterning take place? Because mind not only envisages; it evaluates and enjoys. It identifies certain possible states as good, that is, as desirable and to be enjoyed for their own sake. Aquinas says, following Aristotle, that 'the goodness of a thing consists in its being desirable'.[5]

Many quantum physicists accept Hugh Everett's 'many-worlds' theory, according to which many possible states actually exist. Everett proposed this interpretation of quantum theory as a way of accounting for the superposition of quantum states. He saw the world as continually splitting into alternative possibilities, which are laid down by the laws of quantum theory. Other physicists have extended this idea, as it occurred to them that this universe could be rendered less improbable if it was just one of many universes that all necessarily exist. Each universe would have different values for its basic laws and forces. Then this universe, with its very special-seeming set of laws conducive to intelligent life, would be bound to exist.

But how many universes would have to exist to make this universe more likely? Max Tegmark makes the maximal supposition that all possible mathematically configurable states exist that are consistent with quantum laws. This extreme multiverse posits the existence of all possible worlds. And if indeed such a multiverse exists, the existence of this universe is no longer highly improbable. It becomes virtually certain.

Underlying this view is the axiom that mere possibilities, or probabilities (like the probability-wave for an electron, for instance) cannot exist unless they exist in something actual. As Aristotle said, 'Actuality is prior to potentiality.' We can only speak of possibilities existing if they exist in something actual. So Tegmark thinks of every possibility as actually existing. This in some sense is meant to reduce the otherwise vast improbability of this cosmos existing, out of all the possible alternatives allowed by quantum theory. But another model, and a very natural one, is to think of all possibilities as existing, not in objective reality but in the mind of God, the cosmic consciousness that underlies all mathematically describable possibilities.

Such a mind would know what states are desirable or undesirable. For example, a cosmos containing intelligent life-forms is desirable, but a cosmos in which such life-forms suffer intensely for no reason and without alleviation is undesirable. It would be a very good reason for making a possible cosmos actual that it realises many desirable states, including many finite instances of conscious understanding, appreciation of beauty, moral and creative effort, friendship and happiness.

For Aquinas, there are two basic sorts of reasons that could explain why a specific universe exists. One is set out in the first three 'ways'. It appeals to necessity, to the fact that there has to be an eternal and changeless being with just the nature it has. There has to be a cosmic mind containing the exhaustive set of all possible states. I have shown that this is not some sort of antiquated and arbitrary idea. It is an idea that appeals to cosmologists, as well as to physicists like Einstein, who wrote:

> The aim of physics is not only to know how nature is and how her transactions are carried through, but also to reach as far as possible the utopian and seemingly arrogant aim of knowing why nature is thus and not otherwise ... thereby one

experiences, so to speak, that God Himself could not have arranged these connections in any other way.[6]

But the other basic reason for explaining why things are as they are is to show that they are desirable to a rational being. I explain why I eat ice cream quite well when I say that I like it! I explain why people try to get money by showing that money can get them what they desire. For Aquinas, knowledge, power, friendship and happiness, are all objects of rational desire. They are intrinsically good, good in themselves and for their own sake. Thus I can explain why a specific cosmos exists by showing that it realises intrinsically good things or states.

Aquinas' fourth and fifth 'ways' point to such a form of explanation. They are framed in a way that requires a sympathetic understanding of Aristotelian modes of thought, and these are easily parodied. Richard Dawkins amusingly parodies the fourth way, that all perfections (intrinsic goods) must pre-exist 'in a higher manner' in their causes, by remarking that, since all smells must exist in God, God must be 'a pre-eminently peerless stinker'.

Aquinas, however, does not think that God, who is pure Spirit, actually contains any physical properties, even of stinkiness. He thinks that if an intrinsic good (like human consciousness) comes into being, and if it is to be properly explained, it cannot just 'emerge from night', as Aristotle puts it, from pure nothingness. Either it is necessary, or it comes to be because it is envisaged as good by some being that is itself necessary, and that causes it to exist precisely because it is good.

That 'envisioning of goodness' is not a physical process. It exists in the mind of God. The explanation of a good state is that it is envisaged as a desirable possibility in the cosmic mind, which then seeks to actualise it. It is in that sense that all perfections pre-exist in a higher manner, as ideas in the mind of God. The appeal is to explanation in terms of value and purpose – the universe is brought to be for the sake of the goodness it makes possible.

Dawkins does not seem to accept this as a form of explanation, since in his book *The God Delusion*, when he refers in passing to a previous exposition of this form of explanation by me, he simply says that 'Ward mistakes what it means to explain something.'[7] Perhaps, however, the mistake is not mine. Explanation in terms of intrinsic goodness, desirability and intention is familiar and perfectly respectable, and it does not seem to be reducible to explanations in terms of physics or natural science. Aquinas' explanation of the universe appeals to explanations in terms of both necessity and goodness. God is that mind that necessarily conceives all possible states (a sort of many-possible-worlds theory), and sees some of them to be good. Eternal and changeless mind causes temporal and changing things to be, because they express and imitate the perfect goodness of that which necessarily contains all perfections.

This God is simple, in the sense that it is indivisible, without component parts into which it can be decomposed. The model for such simplicity is consciousness, which may have a rich and complex content, but which is indivisibly one, holding all its complex content together in the indissoluble unity of one consciousness. I suppose Dawkins rejects this idea because he does not think that consciousness, even the pure consciousness of cosmic mind, can exist without a complicated physical basis.

That is just a dogma of materialism. Neither Aristotle nor Aquinas were materialists. They both believed that the ultimate reality, in which alone a complete explanation for the universe can be found, must be mind, a mind uniting necessity and goodness in itself. Aquinas' demonstrations of God seek to support that belief. One would hardly expect his thoughts to be acceptable without modification many centuries later. But they are supreme intellectual achievements of their age. They are today being re-visited by state-of-the-art science in cosmology and quantum physics. And even today it can be quite reasonably suggested that they provide a coherent and plausible exposition of what a wholly intelligible universe would be like. It would be a universe founded on the eternal and changeless reality of perfect mind.

That is the most basic form of theological explanation. What it shows, at the very least, is that appeal to God is not giving up on explanation. Quite the reverse, appeal to this sort of God is the attempt to press reason as far as it will go. If it is mistaken, it is because it presses reason too far, and sees the universe as too rationally structured. It is not because it is some sort of irrational and blind faith. To suggest such a thing would merely demonstrate that Aquinas had not been properly read. And that is one good reason why Aquinas is worth reading rather carefully, and why not every sort of faith should be opposed to reason. Faith, in Aristotle and Aquinas, is precisely faith that reason can disclose the truth about the universe, because the universe is rational, and dependent on a being of supreme rationality or wisdom. It would be absurd to say that such a faith was irrational.

Chapter 3
∞∞∞∞∞∞∞∞∞∞∞∞∞∞∞∞∞

WHY DOES EVERYBODY HATE CARTESIAN DUALISM?

If there is one philosophical view that is almost universally disparaged in the modern world it is 'Cartesian Dualism'. Everyone knows it is wrong, and some philosophers are scandalised by it. 'Dualism must be avoided at all costs', writes the American philosopher Daniel Dennett.[1] And most psychologists and neurologists, even when they talk about and seem to admit the existence of consciousness and its contents – dreams, images, sensations, thoughts and feelings – hasten to add, 'But of course I am not a Cartesian dualist.'

This is very sad, because Descartes was trying to respond to the scepticism of writers like Montaigne, who held that we could not know anything. He was trying to find at least one thing of which we could be absolutely certain. As we all know, he found it in the proposition, 'I think, therefore I am.' But the modern world not only finds it possible to doubt that proposition. It completely rejects it as incoherent.

I will say straight away that I am not part of this modern world. I find Descartes' arguments convincing. But I have to say that furtively, for fear of the scorn of my philosophical colleagues. 'No wonder that man became a theologian,' they say. 'He was, after all, a Cartesian dualist.' However, there is no safety in theology either, since most theologians also have nothing good to say about Descartes. 'Humans are psycho–physical unities', says one of the most respected physicists and theologians, John Polkinghorne. And he contrasts his own position, of 'dual-aspect monism', with dualism. Dualists, it seems, are hard to find.

And yet there are more of us than you might think, lurking in the philosophical undergrowth. And I want to do what I can to retrieve Descartes' reputation. Let me start by making it quite clear that Descartes did think that humans were psycho-physical unities. 'I am not present in my body merely as a pilot is present in a ship,' he says in the Sixth of his *Meditations on First Philosophy*. 'I am most tightly bound to it, and as it were mixed up with it, so that I and it form a unit.'[2]

Humans are compounds of mind and body, and it is not natural or proper to them to be anything else. Plato did think that souls might live a more perfect existence if they escaped from their bodies. Descartes did not. Descartes was a Catholic, and there is no reason to think that he disagreed with Aquinas' view of the soul, which was that every intellectual soul is the soul of a particular body, and is incomplete without it.

So is Descartes a dualist at all, rather than a dual-aspect monist? It would seem very odd to call the 'Father of Dualism' a non-dualist. But we must be quite clear that he thought humans were compound unities, not just composed of two contingently connected and pretty self-sufficient parts. Perhaps an analogy, though not a perfect one, would be water, which is a compound of hydrogen and oxygen, but is nevertheless a compound unity. It could be dissolved into its parts; but if it were, it would be no longer water. So if a Cartesian body and soul were separated, it would no longer be a human being. It would be a dead body and a grievously immobilised and isolated soul. To be a disembodied soul is not a desirable fate, and Descartes did not desire it.

One of the most interesting indicators of Descartes' real view of the matter is to be found in a letter he wrote to Princess Elizabeth of Bohemia on 28 June 1643. Descartes writes: 'I would ask your Highness to hold yourself free to ascribe "matter and extension" to the soul; for this is nothing else than to conceive the soul as united to the body.'[3] Descartes certainly wants to make a distinction between consciousness and extension, and to say that these are two different parts of the soul. The distinction marks two importantly different sorts of properties. But

Why Does Everybody Hate Cartesian Dualism?

this quotation makes it quite clear that he does not want to say that soul and body are two quite different substances which are connected only through some relatively external causal law. Extension – that is, all bodily properties – can be considered as a property of the soul. Descartes, too, thinks of the human person as a 'psycho-physical unity'. He is not the sort of dualist many people think he is.

One other thing that Descartes was certain of – and it was a certainty he shared with the other classical 'Rationalist' philosophers, Leibniz and Spinoza – was that the ultimate reality is not material. The Rationalists rejected old Scholastic modes of thought, and distanced themselves from the traditions of Aristotle and Aquinas. They wanted to clear away the baggage of traditional philosophy, and start again from a newer, firmer basis. The model was the new mathematics, and the aim was to find a wholly rational analysis of the nature of reality, starting from intuitively clear axioms and proceeding by closely argued stages to a complete description of the world.

They were looking for a 'Theory of Everything', a set of necessary truths from which all the laws of nature, and in the end even all the particular events of nature, could be derived. Many modern cosmologists have the same goal in mind. Modern science, and especially mathematical physics, suggests that the basis of perceived reality lies in a set of very precisely integrated mathematically describable laws. If we could trace those laws back to their ultimate root, we might find that there is just one set of consistent laws that generates exactly this universe by necessity.

A favoured candidate in modern physics is that universes – perhaps only this universe or perhaps many other universes too – originate by quantum fluctuations in a vacuum. There might be just one set of consistent quantum laws that generate universes by some sort of internal necessity.

There are great problems with such dreams, not least that the universe seems to be contingent in many of its details, and that there seems to be more than one necessary set of mathematical axiomatic systems. As I mentioned in the previous chapter, the best that Steven Weinberg came up with was that there may be just one consistent logically isolated mathematical theory that is compatible with the existence of intelligent beings. That would be an impressive finding, for it would show that intelligent beings could only exist in a universe like this. But how could we know that there are no possible intelligent beings of quite a different sort, as yet unimagined by us? Or why should that logically isolated theory exist, as opposed to many other possible theories that would not be compatible with intelligent life?

One recent hypothesis is that every possible mathematical theory exists, and all the actual worlds they can produce are produced. We are in just one of those universes. There may be many other universes, some of them with other sorts of intelligent beings, and some with no complex organic forms at all. But we still have the question of where or in what sense mathematical theorems actually exist, and of how they give rise to actual, physical universes.

One thing is clear. In these scenarios, we have moved far beyond saying that the ultimate reality is physical – consisting of points or particles in one unitary space-time. We have moved into a realm beyond any space-time, from which all space-times are generated. Matter, in Descartes' sense of extension and location in public space, is not ultimate. It springs from a transcendent sphere, which is more akin to a realm of pure, necessary and eternal mathematical truths, and yet which has the power to generate one or more forms of space, time and matter.

Whether or not you call this a realm of Mind, it is certainly not a realm of matter. Possibly Spinoza is the philosopher who comes nearest to the dreams of modern cosmology. The realm of the ultimate, for him, was far beyond what we call intellect and will. It certainly does not know in the way humans do, by observation and discursive, exploratory thinking. It does not will in the sense of choosing between alternative possibilities in order to obtain some purpose yet to be achieved. It is the necessary basis of infinite worlds, and from it every possible world is actualised. All exists by absolute necessity, and all must be exactly as it is. Consciousness and extension, mind and matter, are just two of the infinite modes of that reality, the Ultimate Self-existent Substance.

It would be difficult to call Spinoza a 'dualist'. Some call him a monist or pantheist, since he thinks there is only one substance, which he calls 'God or Nature'. But he thinks that substance has infinite modes or appearances or ways of expressing its necessary nature, so it is a monism with extraordinary internal diversity. Some might call it a substance-monism together with a property-pluralism, an infinite diversity of different properties. Spinoza would have no difficulty in saying that mind and body are different, different sorts of properties. But he would not agree that there are just two basic sorts of properties, or that either of these sorts could exist entirely on its own, as a 'substance' in the sense of something that depends on nothing else for its existence.

Yet while Spinoza denies intellect and will of the primary substance, the whole point of his *Ethics* is to advocate a life of liberation from desire and attachment to individual ego. Liberation is achieved by 'the intellectual love of God'. He spells this out, all too briefly, by saying that 'God is absolutely infinite, that is to say, the nature of God delights in infinite perfection ... accompanied with the idea of Himself as cause, and this is what we have called intellectual love.'[4]

So the cause of all things is infinitely perfect, and delights in that perfection. It is impossible to frame this conception without thinking of the ultimate Substance as conscious and capable of delight, that is, as an intellectual being. Moreover, 'the intellectual love of the mind toward God is part of the infinite love with which God loves Himself'.[5] Delight in the infinite perfection of the cause of all things is an objective reality in which human minds can share, and which in fact they, in their own way, express and manifest.

These are not the words of a materialist or of an atheist. They are the words of someone who thinks that the ultimate reality is best conceived by any fully rational human mind as perfect and blissful, as necessary and eternal, as supremely rational and beautiful. God may not be very like human minds, and may be very far from a supernatural person who chooses to answer some prayers and not others, or who performs special favours to those who flatter Him sufficiently. But God is ultimate, perfect, and immaterial Mind. That, and not some sort of matter or blind energy, is the cause of the universe and its ultimate nature.

In 1656 Spinoza was excommunicated from the Synagogue in Amsterdam. He was felt to have strayed too far from the God revealed in the Hebrew Bible. And indeed one of the consequences of allowing Reason free reign, and of seeking to cast off all old authorities and set all human knowledge on a new basis, was the encouragement of a generally sceptical or at least critical attitude to traditional or literalistic interpretations of holy texts.

Aquinas had found revelation to be a natural completion of Reason's search for truth, and freely submitted to the teaching authority of the Catholic Church. But for the new Rationalists of the seventeenth century, revelation itself, and the interpretation of it by religious authorities, had to be put in question, along with everything else.

The other major Rationalists, Leibniz and Descartes, felt little problem in accepting some form of revelation. Leibniz was a Protestant with a keen interest in Church unity, and Descartes was a Roman Catholic. Descartes wrote: 'The Lord has made three marvels: things out of nothingness; free will; and the Man who is God.'[6]

Yet in their philosophical works revelation does not play a major role, and it is clear that they felt free to interpret revelation in line with their general philosophy. This was no doubt because they agreed that reason shows the ultimate reality to be God, the one and only necessary and perfect Mind, and any true revelation from God could not contradict the findings of reason, which God had implanted in human minds.

There is a slight problem in the fact that the three great Rationalists all knew that their systems were necessarily and deductively certain, and yet they all disagreed with one another. Spinoza knew there was only one substance, that included all things in itself. Leibniz knew that there were an infinite number of substances – 'monads' – but that they were all of the same general sort, having the nature of mind. They do not really causally interact, though they appear to do so: 'Bodies act as though, *per impossibile*, there were no souls; and souls act as if there were no bodies, and both act as if each influenced the other.'[7] In fact, however, all monads change in accordance with purely inner principles or entelechies, and God has arranged them in pre-established harmony. Descartes, on the other hand, knew that there were many substances, all of them causally interacting with each other, but that they fell into two different basic kinds, minds (souls) and bodies.

Something must have gone wrong somewhere! Having the advantage of hindsight, it is not too difficult for us to say what it is. Reason alone cannot give definitive answers to questions about what is real. Reason drives us to seek as many explanations of the world as we can, but when it comes to really ultimate explanations, it seems to arrive at a set of incompatible alternative possibilities, between which it is unable definitively to decide. For example, reason cannot decide whether everything is necessarily what it is (the thesis of determinism, espoused by Spinoza), or whether some things are contingent and could logically have been otherwise (Leibniz's preferred alternative). It cannot decide whether humans have free will, or what exactly it would mean for them to have it. It cannot decide whether consciousness is the ultimate reality or not (all the Rationalists agreed that it is). It cannot decide whether ultimate Mind, if there is one, has revealed anything reliably or not. It cannot decide whether the universe is finite or infinite. And it cannot even decide whether the universe is objectively rational or a product of chance, 'born of night', in Aristotle's phrase.

That does not mean that reason is useless. It means that reason alone cannot definitively resolve ultimate questions about human and cosmic being. One of the consequences of philosophical Rationalism is that its failure to arrive at agreement on what a purely rational universe is like has made us now less confident of what reason can do. That does not make reason less important. Reason demands that we should seek to make our knowledge as comprehensive as possible, make our beliefs consistent and compatible with the best available knowledge, and be prepared to justify those beliefs in some intelligible way. What we cannot do is pretend that reason alone can resolve all the really deep questions – questions, especially, of the nature of ultimate reality, of the nature of the human person, and of how to live well.

Descartes stressed clarity and distinctness as the marks of rational knowledge. But there are many aspects of human experience, and ones that he drew attention to, that resist clear description and analysis into distinct and isolatable parts. In the colourful and value-rich field of personal experience there are forms of understanding that require discernment, judgement and empathy, rather than the dispassionate objectivity that is supposedly characteristic of experimental science. The methodology of the natural sciences may well turn out to be inadequate for the understanding of human consciousness. Yet both the material world and the world of consciousness require the use of reason, and that in turn requires that sensitivity as well as clarity should be involved in the use of reason.

Careful attention and sensitivity is needed, and a lively sense of the frailty of human thought, if we are to have any hope of arriving at an adequate metaphysical view. In the study of physical phenomena, close observation and repeated experimentation is essential. The natural sciences have built up a cumulative body of knowledge that is well established and firmly founded. But the natural sciences tend to ignore all questions of value, as lying outside their purview. Since the idea of purpose is the idea of processes aiming at states of value, purpose is inevitably excluded along with value. And for that reason the fact of consciousness, of subjective experience, which desires and enjoys values and appears freely to create purposes and goals, remains a problem for natural science. There is no satisfactory scientific way of explaining the fact and nature of consciousness in terms of publicly observed brain-states or behaviour.

This is Descartes' main point. Phenomenal states – sensations, feelings, and thoughts – can be distinguished from physical states. Further, many mental states are what he calls 'intellectual acts'. Some thoughts may seem to just come to me. But I can also actively think, direct my attention, and work hard at extending a train of thought in new directions. This sense of agency, of bringing something about by an effort of attention and will, leads me to say that there are not merely thoughts occurring; there is an agent who – sometimes, if not always – actively thinks.

It does not follow that in any person it is always the same agent who thinks. It is possible that there could be many agents of bits of thought, especially if an agent is identifiable with a specific part of the brain. Yet the continuity of memory and intention, by which 'I' remember what I set out to do years ago, and resolve to continue to do in future, strongly suggests some form of agent-identity within one consciousness. I am the same agent who possesses a continuous chain of overlapping memories, experiences and intentions, which has been modified over time, at least in part, by my past acts.

Having distinguished thoughts, which have no extension or observable location in public space, from physical, spatially locatable and publicly observable properties, and having posited a continuing agent who thinks, the question for Descartes is: can thoughts exist without extension? Can there be conscious states occurring without any physical states?

For him, the answer is clearly 'yes', for in God he already has a paradigm of consciousness without extension. And if thoughts can exist without matter, then a mental and immaterial agent could logically exist also. Perhaps human thoughts never as a matter of fact exist without brains. But perhaps logically speaking they could, and in God they do, or something very like them, some sort of conscious state, does.

Human thoughts, however, seem tied to material realities in a special way. For thoughts are about physical realities, and are formulated in languages learned in social, physically embodied, communities. This strongly suggests that human souls are truly and properly physically embodied. Nevertheless, according to the Catholic faith that Descartes professed, they also have a natural affinity with the non-physical reality of God, in conscious and loving relation to which their final fulfilment lies. It also seems obvious that human souls may be embodied in different material forms, since each human life has progressed from infancy to old age in many different material forms. Of course these forms – from small flexible bodies to large disintegrating bodies – are connected in a continuous chain of gradually changing organic shapes and sizes. Yet such a chain is a contingent reality, and there might be breaks in the chain, larger discontinuities, or greater variations in bodily forms inhabited by the same continuing soul.

Descartes does not seriously propose these as facts. He proposes them as logical possibilities. A soul could logically, like the man who turned into a beetle in Kafka's novel, *Metamorphosis*, find itself in quite a different body. In our world that would be quite a surprise, especially for our husbands and wives. But it is easy to imagine a world in which it happened fairly regularly. And that is all Descartes is really concerned to say. He does not seriously think, being a Catholic, that souls move into new bodies in our world, or that souls ever exist entirely without body in the world to come. He believed, after all, in the resurrection of the body.

The important point for Descartes is that in the psychophysical unity which is the human person, conscious agency has ontological and causal distinctness. The soul is not merely a chance by-product of physical processes, even though it may emerge from physical processes (as we now know, by evolution). The soul is a distinctive sort of reality, and has some causal efficacy, even though the forms this takes are conditioned and limited by the physical processes within which it exists.

That is sufficient for Cartesian dualism. There are many Cartesian beliefs that we may feel unhappy with – the idea that nature is a machine, that animals do not have consciousness, that the pineal gland is the causal link between conscious, phenomenal states and the physical world. There are unresolved problems about how conscious states causally affect physical states. On the other hand, we may in the end have to say that all causal connections just have to be accepted as facts, and that physical causal laws are not so tight and complete as to exhaust all possible causal connections.

The causal laws of physics may be loose enough to permit causation by conscious states in suitably complex physical contexts like brains. It may even be that a complete causal account of nature would have to include forms of purposive and goal-directed causation that are characteristic of conscious minds, but from which modern physics abstracts. We do not yet know enough about the causal bases of physical change to be definite about this, but modern science is much more tentative than it used to be, and seems to have discarded entirely the closed and predictable machine-view of nature that the Rationalist philosophers had to contend with.

There is a basic problem in modern science about the status of value, purpose and consciousness. They have to enter into any complete account of the nature of things, but the natural sciences largely ignore them. One thing all the classical Rationalists agreed about was that value, purpose and consciousness are closely connected and of fundamental and irreducible importance. If human reason is a reliable guide to the nature of things, the ultimate basis of reality must, they thought, lie in a supreme consciousness which unites in itself necessity and value, the inevitability of being as it is and the supreme instantiation of all the values that are found partially and imperfectly in the finite world. From that being the finite universe must originate, whether by Spinozistic inner divine necessity, by Leibnizian 'fulgurations' (literally, lightning-flashes), or Cartesian determinations of unrestricted divine will.

I doubt whether one of these fundamental viewpoints is more obviously rational than the others. Yet humans rightly wish to adopt a rational view, and the question is whether we can arrive at a simple, fruitful, comprehensive, elegant model that can integrate all the various aspects of human experience in one general interpretative scheme. For the classical Rationalist philosophers, any such successful model will be one in which observation and desire, value and purpose, matter and consciousness, form an integrated, coherent and plausible whole.

For some modern thinkers, like E. O. Wilson and Daniel Dennett, this ideal of consilience between what we may call the personal and the impersonal objects of human knowledge is to be achieved by reducing the personal to the impersonal. But that is far from being the only, or even the most plausible, option. A truer consilience would preserve the reality of both personal and impersonal worlds, and integrate them in a compelling way.

Of course, the seventeenth-century Rationalists did not achieve a final true metaphysics. One thing they unwittingly showed was that final truth may be unobtainable by human minds, and that we have to make do with the provisional. But the general form of consilience they suggested seems to me very much on the right lines. In a universe that is intelligible to the extent that this one is, and in which conscious beings capable of aiming at valued goals of action have emerged by the outworking of natural processes, it seems reasonable to posit that nature itself is intelligible and directed towards the realisation of specific sorts of value, which could perhaps have existed in no other possible universe.

If that is so, then the ultimate causal basis of this universe is not blind chance, but an Intelligence which is good, at least in the sense that it contains, envisages, or aims at, states of intrinsic value. This, wrote Leibniz, is a universe which is 'the means of obtaining as much variety as possible, but with the greatest order possible'.[8] Its basis is a blissful and intelligent consciousness, which in some way expresses itself in, but is different from, any space-time or anything in space-time. That, I suggest, is the only dualism Descartes desires. For the highest destiny of humans is to share in that divine consciousness, while also being creatures of dust and desire. If that is Cartesian dualism, I will sign up to it today!

Chapter 4

WHY KICKING STONES CANNOT
REFUTE BISHOP BERKELEY

I have taken it upon myself to defend a number of causes that are currently unfashionable in philosophy. I suppose that, in this respect, my greatest triumph would be if I could resurrect the idealistic philosophy of Bishop Berkeley (1685–1752). I confess immediately that this is probably too much for me. His main contention that matter does not exist seems so contrary to common sense that most regard it as one of the historical curiosities of intellectual history rather than as a serious claimant to metaphysical truth.

Nevertheless, Berkeley always claimed to be a philosopher of common sense, and maintained that he never denied the objective existence of the world when we are not looking at it. His claim was that the external world only continues to exist because God conceives it as existent, and that is not so far from common-sense theism as may be supposed. For do not all theists believe that if God ceased to conceive the universe, it would entirely cease to be?

However, Berkeley's claim is that he can demonstrate that the very idea of a material universe existing without any consciousness of it, whether divine or human, is contradictory. It is the idea of giving such a demonstration that seems difficult, since many people can apparently think of a universe without a creator God. Berkeley proposes to show that the very idea of such a thing is absurd. This is such an extraordinary idea that it may possibly be true.

We have got used to the idea that in modern physics theories about the nature of physical reality are much more extraordinary than we had suspected. One of the founders of quantum mechanics, Niels Bohr, is reputed to have said of a certain physical theory that it was 'not crazy enough to be true'. At least that could not be said about Berkeley.

Perhaps the place to start in considering Berkeley's theory is with the ancient distinction between reality and appearance, as amplified by quantum physics. The ancient theory says that the world as it appears to our senses is not reality as it is in itself. It is reality as it appears to us, and that appearance takes the form it does because our sense-organs and our brains function in the way they do. Our perceptions do not simply copy reality in a simple one-to-one way. They construct images that are doubtless caused by reality, but do not copy it.

A very simple example of this is the perception of colour. Every physicist knows that colours do not exist in the objective world when nobody is looking at things. There are wavelengths of light, a rather small range of which are visible to the human eye. What the eye perceives is turned into electrochemical impulses that are conveyed to a number of areas in the brain, which cause neurons to fire, and produce in us the awareness of different colours. The perception of colour comes at the end of a complex causal chain. Its immediate cause is the firing of neurons in the brain. Its remote cause is the impact of electromagnetic waves on the retinal surface of the eye.

Some neurophysiologists say that the perception of colour is identical with neuron-firing. Even if in some sense that is true, the particular sensation of colour of which the perceiving subject is aware cannot be detected by any public observation or measurement. It is an 'inner quality' of brain-function that could have been otherwise, or might never have existed.

That inner quality is the appearance of colour. Whatever it is, we can be sure that it does not exist when there is no brain, no perceiving subject, and no consciousness. It is not a copy of anything in the external world, though it may be caused by a chain of events in the external world.

That is sufficient to distinguish the appearance, as it is apprehended by a perceiving subject, from non-conscious reality. Colours are the appearances of something; but they are not copies of anything in the material world.

So far we have only made the distinction, familiar to John Locke, between secondary qualities, like colour, sound, smell, touch, and taste, that only exist in some consciousness, and primary qualities, like mass, position, and velocity, that exist whether or not anyone is conscious of them. But now Berkeley issues one of his main challenges: what justifies us in separating primary and secondary qualities in this way? Are primary qualities not just as much appearances to consciousness as secondary qualities?

This is where quantum physics comes into its own. For classical Newtonian physicists, the material world was conceived as an absolute space and time in which there were small massy particles moving around, bumping into one another, and forming surprisingly stable and complicated structures. The quantum world, which has completely superseded the Newtonian world, is very different. There is no absolute space and time. There are no indivisible particles that have definite position and momentum. And the inner nature of the sub-atomic world has become completely unpicturable. It can be described in a mathematically subtle and complex way, but what the mathematical terms might correspond to is completely unknown and apparently unknowable.

We do have 'pictures' of atoms, with electrons circling a central nucleus in little regular orbits. But we know that such pictures are not copies. Electrons are probability-waves, and they cannot be assigned a definite position and momentum at the same time. They only seem to collapse into particles in specific conditions of measurement. Without such designed interferences, they are spread out in a fuzzy sort of way that can be captured with precision by mathematical equations, but that defeats all attempts to make little pictures of what they are like.

Mathematical models describe sub-atomic quantum reality

with precision. But when physicists try to explain what the mathematics corresponds to, they quickly start talking about superpositions, non-locality, mutli-dimensionality, imaginary time, and curved space.

In this situation, quantum physicists adopt a range of diverse attitudes. Some, probably most, say, 'Let us set aside all questions about trying to imagine external reality. Just do the maths. It works, producing amazingly exact predictions and fantastically elegant axioms and complex sets of postulated interactions that explain how things in the observed world happen as they do.'

This is the pragmatic approach, largely adopted by Niels Bohr. There is no point in asking what matrix mechanics corresponds to, any more than there is any point in asking what the square root of minus one – a very useful mathematical device – corresponds to. These equations enable us to explain and predict what happens in observed reality. All we know is the interaction between an unknown reality and perceiving subjects. This interaction, but not the unknown reality beyond it, can be described by postulating various sorts of forces and regular interactions between them.

Just as our perceptions are caused by some reality that is different from them, so our mathematics describes some reality that is almost certainly different from the models we use (because we do not know how to interpret them realistically). There is an unknown external cause. Our mathematics, like our perceptual consciousness, is a tool that enables us to understand the observed world, the world that is the result of an interaction between the unknown cause and the perceiving subject. Further than that we cannot go.

The appeal of this agnostic and pragmatic interpretation may be strengthened when we hear physicists saying that 'imaginary time' is more real than the time we experience, or that as we approach the beginning of our universe, time turns into something more like space, thus obviating the need for a 'first moment of time'.

There is a conflict between realist quantum claims that time is unreal, or that our universe is constantly splitting into parallel worlds, or that we are three-dimensional holograms (all claims that have appeared in respectable physics journals in recent years), and our common-sense belief that we do one thing after another, that we continue to exist in just one universe, and that we are more than holographic illusions.

Scientific realism (the theory that science tells us what the external world is really like) has for most people become too fantastic and counter-intuitive to be taken seriously. Of course we must take the mathematics and the experiments seriously. But perhaps we should resist the temptation to say that unobserved reality is exactly like the current models offered by quantum physics.

We do not have to deny objective reality. We only have to deny that physics tells us exactly what it is like. Mathematical physics provides something like a schematic diagram of how the sub-atomic world acts. But it is at least as unlike the external world in itself as a set of statistics of train-arrivals and departures is unlike a fleet of actual trains arriving and departing.

I think this negative part of Berkeley's case is very much strengthened by quantum physics. It is no longer plausible to say that primary qualities copy external reality (which is a set of billiard balls bumping about), whereas secondary qualities do not. Both observation and mathematics are mental constructs that schematise an unknown causal substructure in its interactions with observing human agents.

It follows from this that matter does not exist, if by that we mean that matter as we picture it does not copy the true nature of the external reality that causes our experience and understanding of the world.

Are we doomed, then, to be forever agnostic about the nature of the external world? At this point Berkeley's more positive argument comes into play. Whatever the cause is, it is the cause of consciousness and understanding. What we know is an interplay between, on the one hand, some unknown external causative structure, and on the other hand, conscious observations and mathematical postulates. It would be equally absurd to drop either the external cause or the element of consciousness and understanding. We seem to be committed to an interaction between external causation and mind.

The main point here is that mind cannot be eliminated from the only understanding of reality that we have. And mind is not just a passive receptor of sensations. It actively engages in the creative, explorative, and deeply rational activity of postulating mathematical axioms and relations, and testing deduced consequences in imaginatively devised experimental situations. As Berkeley held, we have our primary notion of causation in the active causality of mind, as it seeks to understand the universe by deploying its own conjectures and investigations.

Some empiricists have erred by thinking of sense-impressions as passively received imprints from an external source. But scientific understanding of the world requires imagination and activity, the interrogation of the data of consciousness by a mind that searches for intelligible understanding. The extraordinary thing is that it finds such intelligibility, that the structure of the experienced world is such that it is revealed to the enquiring activity of mind. The cause of our perceptions may be unpicturable; but it is deeply intelligible. It seems to have the character of a rational whole, not of an accidental concatenation of chance occurrences. What modern physics reveals is the rationality and beauty of being, rather than the wholly accidental and random character of a non-conscious and non-intelligent set of brute facts that exist for no reason.

This suggests that mind, which generates rational structure and intellectual beauty, may be a fundamental element of the experienced world. Some quantum physicists, most notably John von Neumann, have held that without mind probability-waves do not collapse into actualities. The only fully real things are observed things. Apart from observation, there is only possibility. Werner Heisenberg argued that the unobserved world is a world of 'potentialities or possibilities'. Superposed particles are possibilities of particles being in particular locations if they were to be observed. And John Wheeler held that no phenomenon is real unless it is observed (by which he meant measured by some recording device).

One might think of the situation as conceived by these quantum physicists like this: without observers, the world consists of a shifting set of possibilities-for-being. Some members of this set are 'collapsed' into actuality by observing minds. That establishes a history of actual events that will modify and limit the possibilities that continue to exist. So all actual events are mind-dependent. They result from the interaction of a set of potentialities and the creative activity of minds.

In what sense, though, do potentialities exist? Berkeley never solved the problem of what the world is like when no one is looking at it, except by suggesting that God is always looking at it. This was never a totally satisfactory solution, for it would seem that God has to see things from every possible point of view at once, which seems very odd.

Berkeley noted that God's eternal view of the universe must be very different from the views any finite minds may have of the universe. So when he considered what the universe was like before any finite minds saw it, he proposed that God created the universe as a set of possibilities-for-perception, as something that could be perceived by finite minds if there were any. But, despite his repeated protestations, this does not quite seem like an actual existence of anything at all, much less a universe. It is as though he has to say: 'There is nothing actually there. But there would be if anyone was looking at it.' That is not a fully convincing account of the Big Bang, which seems to have happened, even though there were no finite minds to observe it.

Quantum physics may be able to help Berkeley out a little. If we think of the unobserved world as a set of mathematically structured possibilities, that set must exist in something actual. Possibilities cannot simply exist unsupported in a half-real world between non-being and actual-being. Half-existence is not good enough; you either exist or you do not. Yet it makes sense to speak of possible existents, of real potentialities, that are different from absolute nothingness. Such possibilities could be conceived by a mind that may have some inclination or reason to bring some of them into being.

The sort of actuality in which possibilities may plausibly reside is a mental actuality. Thus we can see the world of potentialities as a world entertained in and supported by a cosmic mind. This world is not absolute nothingness. It has a sort of actuality. It has a mathematical structure, and a dynamic and systematically changing form that can be captured to some extent in such things as Schrodinger equations. But that structure is not independently existent. It only exists, as possibilities do, in an actual consciousness, in the mind of God.

As Berkeley said, the only effective causality of which we are directly aware is the causality of our own minds in enquiring into nature and making ideas into actual things. Consciously apprehended objects are the only real and actual objects there are, and consciously intended objects (first conceived as possible objects and then brought into being as actual objects) are the only instances of actual causality (of one thing actually bringing about another) that we experience.

Thus for many quantum physicists, the external world is no longer material, in any straightforward sense. It is a mathematically intelligible and intricately ordered world of possibilities, potencies, or tendencies to exist. As such it can plausibly be thought to exist in a sustaining consciousness, in the mind of God. Finite minds like ours collapse some of these possibilities into actual histories, and so there comes into being a shared world of consciously perceived and intellectually understood actual objects.

Take away consciousness and intellect, and the world disappears. Take away finite consciousnesses, and this world of more or less solid coloured and extended objects in motion dissolves into a sea of probability-waves in a multi-dimensional logical space. Take away the cosmic mind that holds those fluctuating potentialities in being, and not even the possibility of the world remains. Mind becomes fundamental to being, and matter is a mode of its manifestation.

This, I think, is all that Berkeley intended to convey in his system of immaterialism. When he said that material substance does not exist, he only meant that it is not actual unless some mind conceives or perceives it. With the help of Heisenberg and von Neumann, we may see that the world of mathematical potentialities is not just non-existent. But it is not the solid, picturable thing we may have thought. We cannot picture it at all, though our minds are capable of understanding it by creative and rigorously logical activity. So we most plausibly think of it as having a deeply creative and logical structure. As such, it is most naturally seen as the expression of a creative and rational intelligence, and as having no reality other than that accorded to it by that intelligence, an intelligence that is fully actual, and not merely potential.

Dr Johnson's famous response to Berkeley, which consisted in Johnson's kicking a stone and saying, 'Thus I refute him!', misses the point, if not the stone, completely. Of course stones are actual physical objects, and they feel solid to us. But any physicist will agree that they are not in fact solid, that they consist of minute particles circling in much greater areas of empty space. The particle physicist will add that even particles are probability-waves that only collapse into particles in a measurement situation. So though sensory appearances can hurt, they really are appearances to human minds and senses. They do not exist unobserved.

Berkeley is logically ruthless in insisting that there are no exceptions to this principle. All our knowledge without exception is of appearances. But then he suddenly turns this theory completely on its head. Instead of saying that the appearances are illusions, manifesting a totally unknowable reality that is quite different, he suggests that the appearances *are* the reality, and that it is the idea of an unperceived material substratum that is unreal. Physicists talk about a mathematical substructure, but the substructure of appearances is in fact no more than an abstraction from the full reality that we observe. It is true that there is a mathematical substructure, but it is no sort of independent or 'more real' level of being.

What we see is what there is. But it has no existence apart from observation. All real things are the contents of consciousness – a sentence uttered by one of the most able mathematical physicists of the twentieth century, John von Neumann. The mathematical structures of quantum physics are not the contents of human consciousness, but they are the contents of the universal consciousness that provides the material for finite consciousnesses. 'All the choir of heaven and furniture of the earth ... have not any subsistence without a mind', as Berkeley succinctly puts it.[1]

Is it true that we cannot even conceive of an unperceived object, as Berkeley claims? We always think of objects as they would look to us. We have to add that in quantum physics we think of objects in purely mathematical terms, but we probably have to admit that they are only 'objects' in a very peculiar sense. We certainly cannot picture them. They are mathematical constructs, and we cannot say what those constructs correspond to. They are abstractions or possibilities, modelling a reality that is outside of our minds, and that has a coherent, probabilistically predictable and intelligible structure.

My own view is that, while we know that the external world is not a simple copy of our conceptions of it, we cannot actually deny that there may be an independently existing material world underlying our mathematical models. But we either have to be totally agnostic about the character of that world, or we should say that it most closely resembles the existence of a network of possibilities conceived by a great conscious intelligence.

In science, in other words, we encounter the mind of God, mediated through the intelligible laws of the natural universe, which exist in God as structured potentialities for finite existence.

Berkeley was a Bishop, and he quoted the New Testament in support of his philosophy: 'In God we live and move and have our being' (Acts 17:28). Humans do not exist in an impersonal, mechanistic and purposeless universe. They exist 'in God', for the whole material universe is sustained in being only because it is conceived in the mind of God.

He might have added, from Paul's letter to the Corinthians, that 'In him [Christ] all things in heaven and on earth were created ... and in him all things hold together' (Col. 1:16–17). Christ is the eternal Wisdom (*Logos*) of God, and we might say that Christ is an expression of the possibilities for created worlds, from which this universe was actualised, and within which this universe continues to exist.

Moreover, the purpose of God for the universe is 'to gather up all things in him, things in heaven and things on earth' (Eph. 1:10). Christians have not always taken these statements that the universe was created and continues to exist in Christ, and is to be consciously united in Christ, with full seriousness. The statements imply that the universe is not a material entity separated and apart from God, in which an external God interferes from time to time. On the contrary, the universe is only able to exist because it is part of the mind of God, and all its features express the operations of that mind, in its relation to the minds of finite spirits. In that sense Berkeley's philosophy is an authentic intellectual systematisation of Christian faith.

In our ordinary everyday experience we therefore directly encounter the mind of God, but as partly expressed and partly concealed in the colourful, sensuous complexity of a world whose actuality partly depends upon the choices and attitudes of human and other minds. It is because those choices have been so consistently self-centred and destructive that the presence of God often seems remote or even hostile to our desires and purposes. But we might expect the purposes of God to be realised in the end, at which point the actual history of the world would be perfectly in accord with the intentions of its creator.

Berkeley's philosophy is often misunderstood. He may be right that the only actual beings we can think of are beings-as-perceived or beings-as-conceived in the mind. If we know, as quantum physics suggests, that a 'material' world could not be simply a copy of our perceptions or conceptions, we may be forced into a total agnosticism about what an unconceived world is like. Or we could accept the view of Berkeley and Niels Bohr that there simply is no unconceived world, since we lose little by dropping the idea of a world of which we know absolutely nothing. We can then say that both possibility and actuality are generated by and in minds of various sorts. We actually know the world perfectly well, by immediate acquaintance, though there is always more to discover and learn about it through the use of creative rational enquiry.

Idealism is, in its most general sense, the view that consciousness is ineliminable from the idea of actual existence, and that purposive causality (intentional generation for a reason) is ineliminable from the idea of efficient causality in its full sense. For idealists a world without consciousness and purpose is a purely hypothetical abstraction that is useful for some purposes (for mathematical description and prediction, for instance), but it is incapable of actual existence.

The real world is a world of finite spirits, beings of value-saturated experience and creative purpose, existing within one supreme spirit of unrestricted consciousness and value. Human life is not a pointless flicker of awareness in an indifferent and finally decaying machine. It is a developing awareness by finite spirits (but unfortunately not always developing) of the wider consciousness and purpose of the supreme spirit within which they exist, and with which it is their inherent goal to unite in that blissful state of completed desire that is termed love. This is a very suitable philosophy indeed for a Bishop.

I have defended Cartesian dualism. How can I also defend Berkeleyan idealism? After all, Berkeley disagrees completely with Descartes in denying the independent existence of material substance, the inner nature of which is both unconscious and unknown. But I defended dualism by pointing out that Descartes did not in fact believe that finite minds exist in complete independence of bodies. He believed that minds and bodies form a complete intertwined whole, and that within that whole mental causality plays a vital part. Descartes also believed that material substance could not exist without God, who exists necessarily and is the one and only creator of all matter.

All that Berkeley denies is the existence of matter without mind. He does not deny that matter exists, in the sense of physical objects that are perceptible by finite minds. Nor does he deny that minds that desire to express themselves and communicate with others will always need some quasi-bodily medium to facilitate such desire, even though there may be many kinds of 'bodies'.

While there are important philosophical differences between Descartes and Berkeley, they both agree that mind or spirit is the primary and fundamental form of existence, and that finite minds can in principle exist in different forms of embodiment or publicly perceivable expression. Matter, for Berkeley, is what is perceived, and mind is what perceives. Both exist, and in the case of finite minds, they properly exist together. That, I have held, is just what Descartes thinks, even though he believes that matter does not have to be perceived in order to exist. It is thus possible to defend both Cartesian dualism and Berkeleyan immaterialism, not as a whole, but in respect of some of their most important affirmations. But which do I really accept? Being a tolerant, open-minded, somewhat indecisive philosopher, obviously I accept something in between.

Chapter 5

WHY DAVID HUME IS ODDER THAN YOU THINK

So far all the philosophers I have talked about have agreed that an ultimate and irreducible element of reality is mind or consciousness, and that this consciousness may be the one ultimate source of all reality. If that is so, it will have power to bring about all that exists, and as it is aware of all possible states, and able to discriminate between good (rationally desirable) and bad states, it will itself be a reality of supreme perfection and value. This ultimate reality of supreme power and goodness is God.

Most of the philosophers who form part of the classical canon of Western philosophy have indeed agreed with this general view. But there is a significant minority report, which also finds its roots in ancient Greece, in the writings of Democritus and Epicurus. Rejecting the idea of a supreme Good or of a creator God, they held that everything that exists is composed of atoms, without consciousness, purpose, or intelligence. Human beings, and consciousness itself, are by-products of the complex interplay of atoms. Human existence has no objective purpose, and when all human life comes to an end, all will end as it began, with the ceaseless circling of atoms in the void, unseen and undirected by any mind, human or divine.

It would be churlish to ignore this tradition altogether, and its existence demonstrates the odd fact that humans disagree fundamentally about the nature of the reality of which they are part, and their disagreements seem to be unresolvable by reason. This suggests that the function of reason is to bring out the axioms and implications of general systems of thought that are adopted on non-rational grounds. But reason of itself cannot resolve the ultimate questions of what reality is like, or of how humans ought to live.

That conclusion fits the thought of David Hume (1711–76), the eighteenth-century Scots philosopher who stands firmly in the Epicurean tradition, and whose sustained attack upon arguments for the existence of God is still a major intellectual influence in the contemporary world.

Hume had a low estimate of the place of reason in trying to understand the ultimate natures of things. 'Human understanding', he said, 'is by no means fitted for such remote and abstruse subjects.'[1] What then takes the place of reason? 'Custom is the great guide of human life.'[2] 'Our author concludes', he says of himself, 'that we assent to our faculties and employ our reason only because we cannot help it. Philosophy would render us entirely Pyrrhonian [sceptical], were not nature too strong for it.'[3]

Hume undertakes to show that reason is unable to establish most of the beliefs that we take for granted in our everyday lives. There is no way of proving that the future will be like the past, or that there are necessary causal connections between physical objects. Indeed, reason cannot prove that there are any physical objects, which exist when we are not observing them. It cannot prove that there exist any other minds, which have ideas in them, or that we have free will, or any sort of continuing selves at all. There is not very much that reason can establish.

What, then, are we to do? Hume seems to suggest that we should just follow the 'lively conceptions' we have, that have been produced in us by habit or custom. We must believe what we do believe about external objects, other minds, and the laws of nature, because we cannot help it. We cannot prove or justify any of our basic beliefs, but when we stop doing philosophy, we realise that we cannot get by without them, and so accept them anyway.

This is a very strange recommendation, that there is no point in trying to justify any of our beliefs rationally, so we should just believe whatever is customary or habitual with us. It opens the door to believing whatever our society has taught us to believe, since our habits will be largely socially conditioned. It is a perfect defence of unthinking theism. If Hume had not disliked religion so much, his arguments would provide a complete defence (from his point of view) of religious belief. For belief in God is certainly habitual with many people, and reason is powerless to undermine such a belief.

Accordingly, when Hume wrote his *Dialogues Concerning Natural Religion*, he was only concerned to deny that reason could establish the existence of God. Hume seems logically committed to accepting the argument that belief in God is just as reasonable as belief in an external world, and that we are perfectly entitled to adopt it if it is part of our habitual or common-sense worldview.

It would, however, also follow that any habitual belief is acceptable, as long as we do not pretend to have a rational justification for it. And that might unsettle a theist who thinks that belief in God really is more reasonable than many alternatives. There must surely be some way of distinguishing crazy beliefs, however habitual, from sensible ones. But what could it be? I do not think Hume ever solved that problem. But one possibility is that sensible beliefs are those that are not disconfirmed by experience, that help us to make sense of the 'buzzing blooming confusion' of sense-experience, as William James called it, and that are useful or even necessary to the conduct of life.

That was the argument of Thomas Reid, a contemporary of Hume, who was much better known as a philosopher than Hume at the time and for many years afterwards. Reid was a major proponent of the Scottish 'common-sense' school. He argued that we are entitled to accept common-sense beliefs like the existence of an external world and of other minds, and indeed the existence of God. For it is a natural inclination of the human mind, he held, to think that the wonderfully organised complexity of nature is the product of a wise creator. Belief in God is a common-sense belief. It is not contradicted by any experience, it helps to make sense of the apparent order and complexity of the world, it is confirmed by the experience of a good part of humanity, and it is conducive to moral commitment, and to mental health and well-being. So it possesses the only sort of rational justification that we can ask for in the area of ultimate worldviews.

This is a largely pragmatic defence of belief in God. Such belief is 'useful', insofar as it produces moral action and human fulfilment. But it also expresses Thomas Reid's rejection of Hume's basic philosophy, the 'philosophy of impressions and ideas'. For the fact is that Hume was not, after all, a total sceptic. He had a view of the nature of reality and of human knowledge which was, he thought, more rational than any other.

Hume had an extremely rigorous conception of the nature and limits of human knowledge. When he said that reason had nothing of its own to contribute to human knowledge, he was following, in a much more extreme way – indeed, in the most extreme possible way – the empiricist philosophy of Locke and Berkeley.

John Locke held that 'knowledge seems to me to be nothing but the perception of the connexion and agreement, or disagreement and repugnancy of any of our ideas. In this alone it consists.'[4] For the British Empiricist philosophers, all human knowledge must not only begin with experience, it must be confined to the limits of possible experience. All knowledge must derive from the senses, and it must deal only with the relations between various sense-experiences.

Locke was not consistent in his application of this principle. He allowed, for instance, knowledge of God – who is certainly not a sense-experience – and accepted the existence of an external world of primary qualities, like position, velocity, and mass, as a rational inference from sense-experience. That external world was dispensed with by Berkeley, who argued that if all knowledge is confined to sense-experience (to 'ideas'), and if all ideas are held within some perceiving consciousness, then we have no reason to think there is an external material world. We only have ideas and minds that perceive them: 'to be is to perceive or to be perceived'.

Hume continued to purge knowledge of all but experience by claiming that we do not even have ideas of a perceiving mind. He distinguished ideas from impressions, which are the original data of experience. He then insisted that there is no impression of a substance, the mind, that perceives. There is only a succession of feelings, sensations, thoughts, sentiments and perceptions. For Hume, to be is to be one of a set of contingently connected impressions. There is no longer any 'perceiver' or 'perceived'. There is just a flow of impressions.

All knowledge consists in the 'association of ideas', in a natural association of ideas because of resemblance between them or because of contiguity, the fact that one idea is close to another, or because of a habit of expecting past successions to be repeated (causality). God, the world, the self, the laws of nature, and the existence of successions of impressions unperceived by us (the minds of others), all lie beyond the narrow bounds of knowledge as defined by Hume. This is as far from common-sense as it is possible to go, and common-sense can only be restored, Hume suggested, by putting aside philosophy and playing pool until the fevered philosophical brain has cooled down a little.

I began by suggesting that Hume stood in the Epicurean tradition, but this is only true to a limited extent. Hume, like Epicurus, resolves the whole of reality into simple basic atomistic elements that are connected by chance and accident, and that depend upon no mind that contains them or intends them to be as they are. But for Hume, unlike Epicurus, the basic atoms are not objective unobserved physical entities. They are impressions, contents of consciousness (except that there is no consciousness in addition to the impressions; the consciousness just *is* the collection of impressions). We do not have colourless atoms with position and mass. Instead we have patches of colour, blasts of sound, rushes of sensation, and flushes of feeling, all strung together in an unplanned and accidental sequence. In such a world, it is a miracle that reason can find any foothold at all, and it is not surprising to find that Hume describes reason as 'the slave of the passions'.

It seems to me that there is something wrong with any philosophical theory that leads to such consequences, and that Hume's theory is the *reductio ad absurdum* of radical Empiricism. I agree with Thomas Reid that we are certain that there is an external world that necessarily acts in accordance with general laws of nature, there are other conscious minds and other impressions of which we can have no personal experience, and there is an active and continuous self that reflects upon its impressions and ideas, perceives resemblances between them, and constructs philosophical theories to account for their existence. I am sure David Hume thought so too. Why, then, did he have a theory that reduced rational certainty to mere habit and custom, and pretend that an obscure and radical Empiricism, founded upon highly contentious premises, was actually the certain foundation of all human knowledge?

In short, if Hume was going to be sceptical about the capacities of human reason, why was he not more sceptical about his own dogmatic Empiricism, about the extraordinary opinion that every item of genuine knowledge must be traced back to the occurrence of specific and discrete impressions?

The obvious alternative to Hume's theory is that knowledge does not result solely from the passive occurrence of impressions. Knowledge results from the activity of the mind, considering and comparing its experiences, and imaginatively constructing models that can clarify and explain how and why our experiences occur as they do.

Hume says that we have no impression of a self, so that there is no justification for postulating one. But the self is known precisely in the activity of considering questions like that of whether all our knowledge derives solely from sense-impressions. The self is the active agent that asks what can best account for its experiences. This does not foreclose the question of whether the self is physical or spiritual, a property of the brain or a thinking substance. But it establishes that we have knowledge of the self, not by having a particular discrete impression of it, but by reflecting on the activity of thinking. We find ourselves attending, concentrating, focusing on a problem, to a greater or lesser degree. These are not things that happen to us. They are things we do. And the agent, known precisely in its activity, is continuous at least over large enough stretches of time to enable us to complete a process of thought – so that the same agent who begins a thought-process brings it to an end, perhaps years later.

Knowledge of the self, in other words, derives from reflection on experience, but not from any discrete experience. It derives from reflection on what is presupposed by different sorts of experience, and what underlying, but perhaps unperceived, reality can best account for the experiences we have. The self is a postulate of reason, reflecting on its own nature. If this is so, then Hume is wrong to say that 'Our conclusions are not founded on reasoning or any process of the understanding.'[5]

In opposition to Hume, then, I would say that many of our beliefs are founded on reasoning and reflection, and any adequate theory of human knowledge must admit that fact. The existence of a continuous reasoning self is one of those beliefs. The existence of other similar selves, whose rational activities we do not directly experience, is another. And so the postulate of God, as an agent who perhaps actively envisages and reflects upon all possible worlds, is a postulate founded on reflection. It is a very natural postulate, for the world known to science is highly ordered and mathematically intelligible. The world has a rational structure, and does not seem to be just one random thing after another. It seems to science to be governed by intelligible laws. God might very well be a postulate that explains this fact in a satisfying way.

Knowledge does begin by reflection on experience, and in some way all knowledge must be traced back to experience. But common-sense beliefs are not confined to comparing particular impressions or ideas. They rather postulate an unobserved world of objects in space and time, interacting in accordance with general laws. They also commonly, though not universally,

Why David Hume Is Odder than You Think

postulate that there are objective moral and mathematical truths. And many social groups postulate that there are gods and spirits that can interact with human minds, or that there is one God who is apprehended in prayer, in and through beauty, the intelligibility of nature, the events of personal history, and in revelation through prophets or enlightened sages.

These are reflective postulates that help us to order and interpret experience, and see it not as an accidental sequence of transient and discrete data, but as the impression upon our minds of an external reality that is discernible by understanding, and not by the senses alone.

Modern science departs much further than this from sense impressions and ideas. Quantum physicists speak of electrons as probability-waves in Hilbert space. Particle physicists speak of a ten-dimensional curved space-time in which most of the energy ('dark energy') is completely unobservable. Cosmologists speak of a multiverse, in which different space-times can all exist, each of them originating by quantum fluctuations in a vacuum, a vacuum paradoxically filled with the quantum laws that govern the fundamental constants of many universes, and with whatever it is that becomes, in our universe, a set of amazingly fine-tuned gravitational, electromagnetic, and weak and strong nuclear forces.

Is this almost unimaginable world of which physicists speak the real world? When Stephen Hawking suggests that the universe could be finite in imaginary time but without boundaries or singularities, what sense could Hume make of what he is saying? Hawking says, 'This idea that time and space should be finite 'without boundary' is just a proposal ... like any other scientific theory, it may initially be put forward for aesthetic or meta-physical reasons, but the real test is whether it makes predictions that agree with observation. This, however, is difficult to determine.'[6]

Modern physics is based on reason writ large. It proposes mathematical models that describe a large number of phenomena on the basis of a few simple postulates. These models are so complex that we do not know how to interpret them. Some physicists would not even try. They are partly chosen for their mathematical elegance and beauty. Yet they work. They produce predictions that can be tested – or, as Hawking admits, they sometimes issue in comprehensive models that are very appealing to mathematical physicists, because of the promise that they might unite many diverse phenomena in one relatively simple and comprehensive theory. But we are not yet even very sure how we would set about testing them (as with some versions of String Theory).

It seems to me that physicists are trying to speak of the nature of reality, and that what they have shown is that reality is very different both from what we ordinarily experience (our 'impressions and ideas') and from our common-sense beliefs. It is reason that tells us this, though of course reason has to be tested by experience. That may be very difficult to do in practice, however. Some very general theories, like M Theory, or the Multiverse hypothesis, may only be testable rarely, with difficulty, by few, and perhaps never conclusively. There may be tests that we could never in fact be in a position to carry out.

If you concede so much, it is hard to rule out the postulate of God as quite different in kind from the most general postulates of physics. I am not saying that God is part of physics. Only that the postulate of God is like some postulates of physics, inasmuch as God may be a postulate for helping to understand the nature of experienced reality (where experience may include what seem to be experiences of a transcendent personal reality). The postulate may be in principle testable, since at some far-future time either the universe will achieve the goal of consciously attaining God's purpose, or it will not. In addition, there may be present experiences (of divine grace or of great suffering, for example) that help to confirm or disconfirm the postulate. But the interpretation of such experiences may remain disputable and theoretically inconclusive.

So God is a meaningful postulate, but one that cannot in this life be conclusively confirmed or disconfirmed. This is significantly different from Humean scepticism about reason. For Hume, in his sceptical mood, reason can establish nothing. But on this alternative account, reason can distinguish between comprehensive, fruitful and well-worked-out postulates that have some explanatory force, and postulates that have virtually nothing to be said for them, but rest on blind affirmation. Reason can show, I think, that the postulate of God has explanatory force, though not conclusive force. That suggests that the decisive factor is not going to be pure reason, but the sorts of experiences you have, and the ways of interpreting them that seem most fitting and plausible to you. But reason nevertheless has a vital function in articulating the postulate of God, of refining it in the light of new knowledge, and of drawing legitimate consequences from it in a careful and considered way.

Chapter 6

DAVID HUME'S UN–NATURAL THEOLOGY

In the light of this discussion, what can be said about what has become Hume's classic attack on arguments for God, the *Dialogues Concerning Natural Religion*? I would say straight away that, insofar as the attack depends upon Hume's metaphysics and theory of knowledge, it will lack force, as it would undermine modern science as much as it undermines belief in God. Insofar as the attack depends upon Hume's actual common-sense beliefs, it will justify belief in God as much as it justifies any commonly held belief. Insofar as the attack is upon rational speculation about the nature of reality, it will be self-defeating, since Hume himself speculates about the nature of reality when he publishes what he called his 'proudest invention', the theory that all knowledge must rest solely upon an association of impressions and ideas.

Hume begins the *Dialogues* with his usual complaint that reason is too frail a faculty to decide ultimate questions about reality. 'With what assurance can we decide concerning the origin of worlds?'[1] It is scientific cosmology that gives the reply: with a great deal of assurance. Physicists now routinely publish papers about the originating Big Bang, the accelerating expansion, and the ultimate demise, of our universe. Mathematics is the key to understanding the universe as a whole, and reason does unlock the mysteries of the physical order. Human brains may be small and feeble, but they propound mathematical theories that reveal the structure of the universe as a whole, and narrate its past and future history with confidence.

Hume protests that we can never have any sense-impression of the origin of the universe, so we cannot have any knowledge of it. So much the worse for Hume's theory that all knowledge must be traceable back to some impression. For mathematical models constructed by reason give us knowledge of the origin and end of our universe, and enable us to assess with some precision the probability of its fundamental laws and constants being as they are.

The consensus is that the probability is vanishingly small, and physicists are actively seeking some wider theory that might make the existence and specific nature of this universe less improbable. There are at present a number of candidates that promise to do this. One of them is the existence of a cosmic mind that could envisage all possible universes, and select this one in order to realise some purpose that has great value. Such a hypothesis would make the existence of this universe, a universe that produces intelligent and morally free persons, vastly more probable than it would otherwise be, indeed virtually certain. Any hypothesis that makes the existence of a process more probable is a good hypothesis. Therefore the hypothesis of God is a very good hypothesis indeed.

The problem for physicists is that it is not a hypothesis in physics, since it appeals to a non-physical cosmic mind as its final explanation. Yet it may well be that any truly ultimate explanation will have to move beyond physics, since it will have to include considerations of value, purpose, and consciousness, with which physics does not deal.

This is in fact an additional strength of the God hypothesis. It does not just appeal to order, intelligibility and necessity, the basic values of physics. It also appeals to consciousness, value and purpose, proposing as a reason for the existence of the universe the fact that the universe is consciously aimed at the realisation and enjoyment of distinctive values.

There is deep dispute about whether the universe does realise sufficiently great values to make its existence rationally desirable. Doubt about this accounts for much of the reluctance of some physicists to accept the God hypothesis. There is little doubt, however, that choosing something because it is intrinsically good and desirable is a good explanation for the existence of that thing. I think this is a distinctive sort of explanation – some call it axiological explanation, explanation in terms of value, and some call it personal explanation, explanation in terms of what personal beings might rationally desire. Such explanation cannot be reduced to nomological explanation – explanation in terms of ultimately necessary laws of nature. At least no one has ever proposed any even remotely plausible way in which it could be so reduced. If that is so, axiological explanation would have to be part of any ultimate explanation for the existence of the universe. And this again makes God a better hypothesis than one (like a purely physical one) that omits all mention of consciousness and value.

The major problem is that, while axiological explanation may be a perfectly good and irreducible form of explanation, many people think that it does not look as though it will be of much help in explaining this universe. There is just too much suffering and waste to make it plausible to think that this universe is created for the sake of realising a set of highly desirable values. Or, to put it another way, the values that do undoubtedly exist are outweighed by the suffering and waste that also exist. So an axiological explanation, even if it is possible, will not be a very good explanation of this universe.

Hume naturally raises the problem of how it could be that an omnipotent God could create a universe containing great evils. It is a problem, but it is wrong to suggest that it necessarily shows some inconsistency in the God hypothesis. It could be, for example, that there is a God, a conscious intelligent being who has the greatest power that any being could possibly have, who nevertheless has, by some inner necessity that is real but unknowable to finite minds, to create some universe containing the possibility of suffering and waste, a possibility that even the most powerful possible creator could not eliminate.

It might be that the distinctive sorts of value that exist in this universe could not exist without the possibility of the evils that exist in it, and that some universe rather like this necessarily exists. Believers in God might want to stress that many possible evils need not become actual, and may even be forbidden, though they cannot be excluded, by God. This would be the case, for example, if God's creation included finite persons who could choose freely whether to love and co-operate with other persons or not. This is the classic 'free-will' defence, and I think it successfully accounts for the existence of much actual suffering on this planet. So the universe may in fact contain more suffering than it might or should have contained.

Most believers in God would want to add that all evils can be sublimated or compensated by overwhelmingly greater goods, beyond this life, for all victims of evil. In that case, the balance of good and evil would be greatly modified, and it might be possible to argue that if all lives had the possibility of an overwhelming preponderance of happiness over suffering, the universe could be judged good, and worth creating, overall.

Then we might be able to show that the values of this universe, including the existence of the human species, could not be realised in any other universe. This would in effect be an appeal to a 'final theory', in Steven Weinberg's sense of a theory that shows that the basic laws of this universe are the only ones mathematically consistent with the existence of carbon-based intelligent life-forms.

While attracted by the idea of such a final theory, Weinberg does not think that the value of human life is worth the suffering that goes with it. But if all the sufferings of this life are as nothing compared to the glories that are to come, and if some universe like this simply has to exist anyway, and if we were convinced that we could not exist at all as the persons we are except in this universe, we might indeed say that an axiological explanation could rightly apply to this universe. It could be created for the sake of good, even though it necessarily contains the ineliminable possibility of much evil.

But how can an omnipotent God be bound by such necessities? Hume argues that 'whatever we conceive as existent, we can also conceive as non-existent'.[2] Similarly, whatever we can conceive without self-contradiction, can exist. But we can conceive of evil not existing, and we can conceive of a God creating a world without any evil in it. So evil cannot be necessary, and God did not have to create it. If God did create it, or even allow it, then God is not good.

Hume's argument is that all existence is contingent. Nothing that exists has to exist. There is no such thing as a necessary being, a being that cannot fail to exist. However there are physicists and philosophers who do look for something that exists by necessity, and that therefore would not need any further explanation. For if we could see that something had to exist, that would be a sufficient explanation for why it exists. It could not fail to do so. Some physicists – Einstein for one – look for some sort of necessity that would explain why things are as they are. And most classical philosophers, like Anselm, Aquinas, Spinoza, Leibniz, Descartes and Hegel, also seek to explain the universe in terms of an ultimate being that is necessarily what it is.

According to Hume, however, there cannot be a being that exists by necessity, because we can always conceive of anything as not existing, and thus as being other than it is. What we can conceive must be possible, and therefore any conceivable being whatsoever could fail to exist. Therefore there cannot be a necessary being.

The argument may seem powerful, but in fact it misses the point, because it is due to Hume's mistaken idea that whatever we can picture to ourselves, can exist, that our mental pictures are a reliable guide to what can exist. But this idea contradicts the other Humean idea that the human mind is too weak to conceive of ultimate realities, and that the 'ultimate springs and principles [of nature] are totally shut up from human curiosity and enquiry'.[3] If that is so, we could never know whether some things, including God, exist by necessity or not. We might imagine we can conceive of a world without a God, but the human mind is so weak that we could never trust our imaginations.

David Hume's Un-Natural Theology

I have argued that Hume is too sceptical about reason, and that human understanding *is* a reliable guide to the nature of reality. But there is a great difference between conjuring up a sense-impression or a copy of one and understanding reality conceptually. We may be able to conjure up mental pictures, take some away and add some, and combine them in various ways. But modern physics shows that mental pictures are a very poor guide to the nature of reality. The real world is not a world of colours, sounds, and touches. The real world is a world of Hamiltonians, Hilbert spaces and many unpicturable dimensions. So we have to make a great and important distinction between what we can picture, and what we can understand mathematically and conceptually.

When we ask whether anything could exist by necessity, it is no use trying to call up a mental picture of something, and by concentrating very hard on it, see whether it exists necessarily. Of course we can always wipe the picture out, and say that the imagined thing – be it God or a unicorn – need not exist. But what does that prove about objective, unpictured, and probably unpicturable, reality? Nothing at all!

It is reason that drives us to think of necessity as the ultimately satisfying answer to questions about why things are as they are. We can as a matter of fact think without self-contradiction of something existing, call it X, that could not fail to exist, that exists in every possible world. However, we can also think without self-contradiction of possible worlds that do not contain X. We can think both these things. But they cannot both be so. If the former is the case, then there can be no possible worlds without X. But if the latter is the case, then there can be no being that exists in every possible world, and so X cannot exist at all. It seems that mere thinking cannot decide the issue of whether or not X does, or can, exist.

All we can say is that it seems conceivable that there could be a being that could not fail to exist and be what it is. We can even have a shot at saying what sort of being this might be. For if it is a being that has to exist in every possible world, it is not likely to be a particular object in the world. It could, however, be a being that contains the representations of every possible state of affairs, because if a state is ever possible it will be possible whatever actual world exists. So if there could be a being that is the actual ground of all possible states, it is a good candidate for a being that could exist and be the same in every actual world.

Moreover, if this being is to explain why a universe exists, it will have to contain some principle that selects from all the possible states of affairs a particular world or worlds as actual. If all this makes sense, then I may think I can picture a world without such a ground of all possible states. Indeed, I may think that the very idea of such an abstract ground of all possible states does not make sense. But that may just be because I have not understood fully what is involved in possible and actual existence. Certainly, appealing to what I can or cannot picture is of purely psychological interest, and does not help to decide the issue.

If nature is truly rational, in the sense that there is a reason why everything is the way it is, nature will ultimately be founded on a necessary existent that cannot but be as it is. We cannot picture such a thing, but we can think it. It is a postulate of reason. Of course thought alone cannot decide whether or not such a necessary being actually exists. But necessity may be something that it is sensible and even useful to postulate. Scientists tend to think that there are necessities in nature. Hume in his common-sense mood thinks that there are necessary connections described by the laws of science. The laws of mathematics seem to be necessary, as do the basic principles of morality. So if we can root reality in the necessity of God, who has to be as God is, it is perfectly conceivable that the necessities internal to the divine being are reflected in the general mathematical structure of this universe. It is not our picturing imagination that decides this, but our intellectual understanding, in its conceptual quest for final explanation.

It is because God exists by necessity that the question, 'What caused God?' does not make sense. Beings that exist by necessity need and can have no cause (except in the special sense that a necessary being can be caused by another necessary being). Like mathematical equations, they are uncauseable and unchangeable in their existence and general nature. If we could comprehend them fully, we would see at once why they simply have to exist. So if God exists by necessity, and contains a principle of selecting actual universes (like the principle of selecting them because they realise otherwise unobtainable intrinsic goods), a final explanation for the universe would have been achieved.

Furthermore, if God's essential nature is unknowable in detail by humans, and if God exists by necessity, there might well be necessities in God that humans do not know about, or cannot see the reason for, even though there is such a reason. There may, for instance, be something in the divine nature that necessitates the creation of a universe of free agents. We are in no position to understand what that is. But we can see that even the most powerful possible being would not be able to change that necessity. It is in some such way that God may be bound by necessity, and not be free to create a universe without evil in it, whatever we think we can or cannot imagine.

Of course that necessity will not be external to God. It will not be a constraint on God. It will be a necessary part of the divine nature. So it is not any sort of avoidable limitation on the divine power. God is good, in that God wills the universe for the sake of good, and perhaps wills all personal agents in the universe to have the possibility of overwhelming happiness. God is omnipotent, in that there is no possible power greater than that of God, from whom all other power derives. All this is compatible with the existence of great evil, the possibility of which necessarily exists in God. Some such 'evil' possibilities may be necessarily actualised in any member of a set of worlds of free intelligent agents one or more of which God necessarily creates. Yet the reasons for creating such a world, and the only states of such a world that are directly willed and intended by God, are states of great intrinsic goodness. This, I think, is a coherent response, though it may not be the only one, to Hume's powerful (but hardly original) objections to the axiological postulate that God creates the universe for the sake of goodness.

Hume objects next that a creator God would have to be at least as complex as a universe, and so it would require as much explanation as the universe does. This argument is repeated by Richard Dawkins as though it were conclusive.[4] But again it misses the point. The complexity of the universe is contingent, and the universe is composed of separate parts that did not have to be related in the amazing and wholly improbable, complex and seemingly intelligible ways they are.

God, on the God hypothesis, is necessary, and the ideas of possible worlds that form part of the content of the divine mind are not arbitrarily connected and separate elements. They are the necessarily connected, exhaustive set of all possible worlds, and they are essentially parts of one unitary consciousness that is indivisible and indestructible. It is for that reason that God has been seen by the vast majority of classical philosophers as a coherent final explanation for the universe.

The God hypothesis is precisely that the cosmic mind that selects a universe for the sake of its distinctive values exists by necessity, that all the possible worlds that partly constitute the mind of God are necessarily what they are, and that the necessary connections of things according to the basic laws of physics are rooted in the necessity of the divine mind.

God is not a complex being, made up of separable parts, related to each other in wholly contingent ways. God is a unitary consciousness whose nature is necessary and which is not composed of simpler distinct parts. Therefore God is not complex or contingent in the way that the universe is, and does not require, and could not have, the same sort of explanation as the universe may have. The only proper explanation of God's existence is a demonstration that God exists by necessity. Such an explanation is not available to human minds – the Ontological Argument is an attempt to make it available, but most philosophers accept that, while intriguing, it is not actually a demonstration. Nevertheless, I think the idea that there exists a necessary being having knowledge and intention is a coherent one. We can postulate that there is such a being, whose final explanation would consist in the full exposition and comprehension of its essential nature. That explanation will always remain beyond our powers (as Hume always conceded). But it is still a final postulate of reason that there is such an explanation. And that will make an enormous difference to us, since it will enable us to postulate that the universe is fully rational, and to proceed in science with confidence and in religion with circumspection and humility.

In the *Dialogues* there is, finally, one fatal weakness. Hume saw belief in God as a purely theoretical and weak inference from sense-experience to a cause that bears 'some remote analogy to human intelligence'.[5] More enthusiastic forms of religion he thinks of as 'vulgar superstitions', leading to immorality, hypocrisy and intolerance. Hume was a man of great virtue, even if he had a low opinion of the masses, whom he saw as largely lost in ignorance and folly. His hatred of religion must have had its basis in the real follies and failures of religious individuals and institutions. Of these he was an unceasingly stern critic. But what he did not see or appreciate was that living belief in God is not an inductive inference to an unseen intelligence. It is an encounter with a personal reality that transcends all finite experience, and that proposes a value and purpose to human life that is worthy of unreserved commitment.

A believer in God sees all experience as an encounter, how-ever indirectly, with the mind of the Creator. Belief makes an enormous difference to how life is seen. If you see in morality the inviting voice of a loving God, if you see in the beauties of nature the artistry of a creative spirit, if you see in science the wisdom of a cosmic intelligence, and if you sense in and through all the events of life a presence that seeks to lead you to ever greater life, joy, compassion and courage, then that will, or should, make a great practical difference to your life.

Such living experience is the vital heart of belief in God, and any consideration of reasons for believing in God, even without appeal to revelation, must take account of it. Hume does not do so, but assumes that belief in God is a purely intellectual matter of supposing that there is an intelligent creator of the universe. It is not. Yet intellectual reasoning has to be involved in any attempt to interpret religious experience rationally.

What 'natural religion', as Hume understood it, should add to any alleged interpretation of experience as encounter with a reality of transcendent goodness is an interpretation of such encounter in terms of the God hypothesis, a construct of reason that claims to have explanatory power in terms of ultimate necessity, ultimate causal power, and ultimate value. The hypothesis is not, as Hume supposes, the most minimal inference that we can derive by induction from sense-experience. That might indeed not go far beyond the many competing spirits of some tribal religions. The God hypothesis is put forward as the most compelling integrating postulate that provides a rational interpretative scheme for all the diverse forms of human experience, and that justifies belief, when it does, by the rational basis it gives for those apprehensions of transcendent value and life-transforming intimations of human fulfilment that are the life-blood of religion.

Hume did not have, and did not want, that life-blood. But what I have been concerned to say in this chapter is that Hume's arguments against the rationality of belief in God are far from compelling. They rest largely upon general philosophical principles that would undermine science and common-sense as well as belief in God. And it is worth noting that they do not say that reason can show the non-existence of God. They rather say that reason can show nothing at all – and that is perhaps not entirely reasonable.

It is ironic that Hume, who wished to found all knowledge upon experience, neglected entirely to consider religious experience as a possible source of knowledge. His defence could not be that religious experiences are subjective, private, and not directly accessible to others. For him, all experiences have that character. His main reason for ignoring religious experiences is that they seemed to him, as he said in his *Natural History of Religion*, to be little more than 'sick men's dreams'.[6] Perhaps in the end Hume's comments on religion express his own dislike of religious enthusiasm more than they express a fully reasoned and dispassionate enquiry. But that would be entirely in accord with his declaration that 'reason is the slave of the passions'.

And that is perhaps the most significant feature of Hume's thoughts about belief in God. Hume is probably the greatest of those philosophers who reject the mainstream tradition with regard to God. But part of his greatness, in my view, lies precisely in the clarity and enormity of his mistakes, and in the way they point to the necessity for a philosophy that takes reason much more seriously. Contrary to what is said by some of the philosophically naive atheists of our own day, it is faith that asks for the restoration of reason, and it is the Epicurean hypothesis that threatens to deprive reason of its power, and make it nothing more than the slave of the passions.

Chapter 7

HOW KANT DID NOT UNDERMINE ALL POSSIBLE ARGUMENTS FOR GOD

Immanuel Kant is widely thought of as the philosopher who undermined the possibility of metaphysics, showed that morality is completely independent of religion, and destroyed all rational arguments for God. Yet in fact his aim in philosophy was to set metaphysics on a firm foundation. He suggested that moral obligations would be lacking in all reality, and be unable to motivate our conduct, 'save on the assumption that there exists a supreme being'.[1] And at the conclusion of his *First Critique*, he says, 'Can we ... assume a wise and omnipotent Author of the world? Undoubtedly we may; and we not only may, but must, do so.'[2] That sounds very like an argument for believing in God.

Kant's philosophy is peculiarly complex, but it is completely misunderstood if it is not seen as a defence of belief in one supreme spiritual reality as the ultimate cause of the world. One root of this misunderstanding is a failure to take to heart Kant's distinction between theoretical ('pure') and practical reason.

Kant reports that he had been woken from his dogmatic slumbers by reading David Hume. This did not turn Kant into an Empiricist, but it did bring him to agree with Hume that 'no objects can be represented through pure concepts of under-standing, apart from the conditions of sensibility'.[3] Theoretical knowledge requires both concepts and sense-experiences. Experiences without concepts give no knowledge. But concepts without experiences are 'empty', mere forms of thought without content.

It follows at once that the idea of God has no content, since

Kant believed that no sensory experience or direct apprehension of God is possible. Therefore God cannot be an object of theoretical knowledge. But it does not follow that the idea of God is useless, arbitrary, or merely optional. The idea of God is in fact the supreme ideal of Reason, and the fully rational person has to postulate and assume it.

One way of putting this in a more contemporary fashion is to say that God will never be part of any natural science. God will never be an object studied by chemistry, physics, cosmology, or psychology, and will never be part of any scientific theory. But the idea of God may be a meta-scientific postulate that accounts for the unity and intelligibility of nature, and – even more importantly – that underlies a rational commitment to the pursuit of objective value in morality and aesthetics.

The trouble with such postulates, for Kant, is twofold. They can never be verified, and they often lead to Antinomies, the equal rationality of opposing hypotheses. It was the discovery of the Antinomies, the contradictions, of Reason that led to Kant's Critical philosophy. He thought Reason could prove that time and space are bounded, and that they are infinite; that things are infinitely divisible, and that there must be some smallest indivisible elements (perhaps human selves); that the world is determined, and that the will is free; and that there is a necessary being (God), and that such a being is impossible.

Kant's proposed solution of these polarities is at the heart of his Critical philosophy. It is the doctrine of Transcendental Idealism. All objects of any experience possible to us 'are nothing but appearances',[4] which have no independent existence outside our thoughts. Even space and time themselves are appearances (or the subjective forms in which appearances occur).

Things in themselves, existing apart from our perceptions, undoubtedly exist. But they are completely unknown to us. Kant says that they may be thought as constituting a 'transcendental object', a purely intelligible reality beyond space and time, that is the cause of appearances. It is transcendental because it is posited as necessary by pure reason, not experience. The transcendental cannot be experienced, and is the unknown condition of what we do experience.

The ideas of finite and infinite time, and of simplicity and infinite divisibility in space, apply only to the world of appearances, since the space-time world simply does not exist 'in-itself'. However the ideas of a non-causally conditioned freedom and of a necessary being could, for all we know, be true of the 'real' world. This Kant calls, significantly, the intelligible or 'noumenal' world – significant, because noumenal means 'mind-like'.

Indeed, Kant holds that reason compels us to think of the intelligible world in a specific way. Human agents, in their thought and moral action, must regard themselves as intelligible objects, as not determined by sensibility but by the free use of reason and understanding. As phenomena, humans are determined, Kant thought, by absolute Newtonian laws of nature. But as noumena, as existing in the world of things-in-themselves, humans must regard themselves as free and morally responsible.

Kant says that he has not established the reality of freedom,[5] since realities can only be established by sense-experience. He has not even proved the possibility of freedom, since mere concepts give no theoretical knowledge. Freedom is 'a transcendental idea'. Since there is a transcendental realm, the idea of transcendental freedom does not contradict determinism in the phenomenal realm. The conclusion is that we have no theoretical knowledge that we are free; we cannot prove it, or even its possibility, theoretically. But reason compels us to assume that we are free, as a condition of moral action and rational thought.

Reason also compels us to posit, in the noumenal realm, a necessary being, which is the unconditioned source of all appearances. In the phenomenal world there is no such necessary being. In the intelligible world we cannot know that there is. But reason leads us to postulate an unconditioned non-empirical reality as the cause of the world of appearances. Reason allows, or even compels, us to make this theoretically 'optional assumption'[6] of a necessary unconditioned being, that cannot be shown to be impossible.

At this point what Kant thought of as his distinctive contribution to philosophy begins to loom through the fog: 'I have found it necessary to deny knowledge, in order to make room for faith.'[7] Speculative reason must be deprived of all claims to transcendent insight, so that practical commitment to moral and intellectual agency and responsibility are the true bases of regarding the noumenal world as spiritual in nature, as forming a 'Kingdom of Ends', of free moral persons in community, under one sovereign Author of the universe.

So Kant aims 'to deprive metaphysics, once and for all, of its injurious influence', and to silence all objections to morality and religion forever by the clearest proof. We may find it hard to agree that his proof is very clear. It has been argued over ever since. But it seems that his ultimate appeal is to common sense, to human dissatisfaction with what is temporal, to human consciousness of duty, and to a human sense of the order, beauty and providence displayed in nature.

It is with this general background in mind that we must approach Kant's treatment of the proofs of God. We can predict that he will think no theoretical proofs are possible. He will also think no disproofs are possible, and will argue that Reason will tell us how we are to think of the noumenal world, if we are to be practically committed to the active pursuit of truth, beauty, and goodness. Arguments for God will be important, as setting out how we must think of God if we are to do justice to our nature as rational and moral agents. But they will not convince all reasonable people, since the ultimate grounds of belief or disbelief lie elsewhere than in pure reason. They will not lead to 'unconditional submission', or lay out their conclusions with 'apodeictic certainty'.[8]

Far from undermining all possible arguments for God, Kant's main aim is to defend arguments for God by putting them on a firm and unshakeable basis for the first time. Some presentations of Kant's philosophy portray him as one who destroyed all reasons for believing in God, but then, as an afterthought, added a patently lame defence of God, freedom and immortality in order not to shock his manservant Lampe. That is as far from the truth as you can get.

Kant says of what he calls the 'physico-theological proof' that it 'can indeed lead us to the point of admiring the greatness, wisdom, power, etc. of the Author of the world, but can take us no further'.[9] But how much further would we wish to go? Kant finds in the order and intelligibility of nature such a clear indication of the wisdom and intelligence of the unknown cause of nature that 'the belief [in a wise Author of nature] acquires the force of an irresistible conviction'.[10] He finds in our commitment to obeying the categorical commands of duty a sufficient reason for postulating that our existence as moral beings transcends the world of appearances that our senses disclose to us. And he finds in the 'Copernican hypothesis' that appearances must conform to human understanding, a testimony to the fact that the reasoning self is sovereign over the whole world of sensibility, and gives assurance that noumenal reality is indeed rational and intelligible.

These are Kant's proofs of God, freedom and the transcendence of the self over the world of space and time. They are, he submits, practical rather than theoretical proofs. They are rooted in our practices of seeking intelligible unity and purpose in nature, of moral commitment, and of reasoning and reflection. They give no theoretical knowledge of the noumenal world, since they cannot be verified by sense-experience. They are always qualified by the agnostic consideration that the noumenal world is unknowable. Nevertheless, they disclose how reason commands us to think of that world, even though the way we think is regulative – having its main use in directing our actions in this phenomenal world.

So Kant points out that the physico-theological argument is not deductively inescapable. We could object, as David Hume did, to making analogies between human artefacts and the universe as a whole, or to assuming that the cause of nature must have an understanding and a will analogous to ours. Yet these assumptions are natural conjectures, and better than any others we can conceive. They are certainly good reasons for believing in a wise Author of nature, even if not absolutely compelling.

What they do not do, he says, is lead us beyond the idea of an architect or designer of matter to the idea of a creator of matter. They do not lead to the idea of one necessarily existing first cause (or ultimate explanation) of the world. For that we need to add the cosmological argument, from the contingency of the world to the necessity of its ultimate cause.

Kant's main argument here, already outlined in the Antinomies, is that 'necessity' and 'contingency' are concepts that only properly apply to the world of appearances. So they cannot give knowledge of the noumenal world. But we can, and perhaps must, *think* of the unknown noumenal world as founded on a necessary being, and we must do so, if we are to account for the intelligible origin of the phenomenal (mind-dependent) world in a way that satisfies the demands of reason.

What Kant has in effect done is to bar any claim that Reason has power of itself to prove what noumenal reality is like. But he retains and defends the claim that, *if* the intelligible world is rational (which we cannot demonstrate), *then* it must be founded on an ultimate necessity. The rationality of reality is a postulate of reason, and one that has practical utility, especially in commitment to rational reflection and moral responsibility. If reality-in-itself is not as we think it, then it remains the case that we must at least think it like that. And that is a strong reason for trusting such thoughts, which are themselves the product and direct expression of the intelligible world.

So far there is no indication that Kant is destroying all reasons for believing in God. Quite the contrary, he is admitting some reasons to be natural and convincing, on condition that we postulate that reality is rational, and that we do not mix up metaphysical and scientific procedures, and misuse our metaphysical beliefs to try to dictate the results of scientific investigation.

But now comes the section that has misled many people, and caused them to take a more negative view of Kant. He argues that the physico-theological argument depends upon the cosmological, to get from a designer to a necessary creator. Then the cosmological argument depends upon the ontological, to get from an unknown necessary being to the all-perfect being of religious belief. But the ontological argument fails – so it seems that all the arguments must fail.

Things are not as bad as that, however. It is true that Kant sets out to refute the ontological argument, as it is found in Descartes and in Christian Wolff, a philosopher who had early influence on Kant. They held that in God essence and existence are identical, so existence is included in the definition of God. If God is all-perfect, God will possess every property that it is better to possess than not. But it is better to exist than not. Even more compellingly, it is better to exist necessarily, so that you cannot be created, injured, or destroyed, than only to exist contingently. So an all-perfect being will exist by necessity; there will be no possible world in which it does not exist. It follows that if such a being (a being that exists in all possible worlds) is possible, then it exists in every possible world, and therefore it exists in this world.

This argument is a good test for whether you are really a philosopher. If it seems like verbal trickery, then you are not a philosopher, and you should do something more useful. But if it seems irritatingly convincing, then you are a philosopher, and you are condemned to agonise about problems that most people have never even heard of for the rest of your life.

Kant was obviously a philosopher. He made two main points about the ontological argument. First, it is virtually impossible to think of a being that could not fail to exist. Think of any being at all, even God. We can always imagine that being failing to exist. Huge numbers of people actually believe that God does not exist. Are they thinking a self-contradiction?

Second, you may include 'existence', or even 'necessary existence', in the concept of God. But it does not follow that the concept is instantiated, that there really is a God. Kant puts this rather misleadingly by saying that existence is not a determining predicate, whereas it obviously is. To say that Socrates existed is to say something about Socrates. It is to say that the idea of Socrates was exemplified in space and time. Yet even if we include 'being exemplified in space and time' in the idea of Socrates, it does not follow that Socrates ever really existed. Conceptual possibilities, however fully spelled out, do not entail physical or real existence. So we may say, 'Existence is part of the definition of God', but it will not follow that God exists in reality.

I think these points are basically correct. We cannot be sure that a necessary being is possible. But, as Kant would say, we cannot be sure that it is not possible. We can frame the idea of a necessary being. We can say that we have to posit one, if we are to think of there being an ultimate explanation for the world. But we cannot be sure there is such an explanation, or even that there could be one. It remains a postulate of reason. So the fact that we can insert 'necessary existence' into the definition of something does not show that such a property is really possible, let alone that it is instantiated.

What follows from this, however? Does this show that all arguments for God depend on the ontological argument, and since that argument fails even to show the possibility of God, much less the actuality of God, it follows that all arguments for God are doomed to fail? It does not. The thought that it does points to something very misleading about the way in which Kant deals with the arguments for God.

He insisted that there are only three possible arguments, and he justified this by dividing them into arguments from particular features of the world (the physico-theological), from the world in general (the cosmological), and from concepts alone (the onto-logical). That seems very neat. But it is obvious that there might be very different features of the world that we could consider. There is the order and intelligibility of the laws of nature, the purposiveness and directionality (or otherwise) of cosmic and biological evolution, the occurrence of personal apprehensions of God (notably missing in Kant), the interpretation of moral obligations as objective and categorical (strongly present in Kant, but strangely not considered as theoretical, because not scientific), the sense of providential guidance or inspiration (also absent in Kant, who was very suspicious of such things), and the existence of consciousness, understanding and reason as pointers to the need for a distinctively axiological or personal form of ultimate explanation.

When it comes to considering the world in general, there is not only the contingency of all finite things, but also the dependence of the whole phenomenal world upon mind, and so, it would seem, upon a supreme mind-like reality. This forms the core of Kant's transcendental idealism, but oddly it does not explicitly occur as an argument for God. So it seems that there are more than three sorts of argument to a cosmic consciousness of supreme value. Furthermore, the arguments are not related in a sequential way, so that they all depend on one ultimate argument for their force. Much less do they depend on the ontological argument, which is probably the weakest of all.

Where, then, does the ontological argument occur in all of this? It does not occur at all, as a proof of God. It does, I think, demonstrate that a perfect being, if such a being is possible, would be a necessarily existent being. But the idea of a perfect being (a being of the highest possible intrinsic value) is a postulate suggested (but not entailed) by the convergence of a number of other considerations.

The argument from intelligibility and order suggests a being of great intelligence. This in turn suggests consciousness and purpose, since intellectual action aims at some worthwhile goal. So we have the idea of intrinsically desirable values, also implied by the apprehension of objective moral principles that specify the values of free intelligent action. The physico-theological argument points to an intelligence that aims at intrinsic values, and reason drives us on to ask what could account for this intelligence and the objectivity of those values.

The search for ultimate explanation suggests not only a being that is unconditionally necessary in existence, but a being whose existence explains why the contingent universe is as it is. The idea of a wholly explanatory cause of the world suggests a being with the power to bring about good states and the knowledge of all possible good states. It is not only necessary, but the ground of all possible states, and of the power to actualise some of them for a good reason (because they are of intrinsic value). It will therefore actualise in itself the highest possible values. It will be the most perfect possible being.

These considerations prompt the idea of a necessary consciousness of supreme value, as the hidden reality of which this phenomenal world is the appearance. If we cannot establish its existence theoretically, it is at least how we must think of the unknown reality that is the cause of the whole world of appearances, if we are to think of reality as rational. And we already know, if we accept Kant's Copernican revolution, that the phenomenal world as a whole has to conform to the requirements of rational consciousness. So, without needing to argue that the ontological argument is valid, we have a sufficient ground for the postulation of God in the Kantian hypothesis of transcendental idealism, and in his postulation of the sovereignty of understanding and reason over the phenomenal world of space, time and sensory experience.

Yet the whole Kantian philosophy of transcendental idealism suffers from a deep instability. Kant divides reality into the noumenal, of which we know nothing, but of which we think much, and the phenomenal, which we directly experience, but know to be merely the appearance of something else. It is not surprising that some of his successors simply dropped the idea of a noumenal world, and left Kant as an Empiricist nostalgically longing for the lost quasi-Platonic world of his youth. Most of his successors, in Germany and later in Britain, took a different line. They thought that what was wrong with Kant's view was that it posits an intelligible world that is the cause of this one, and yet it claims that nothing at all can be known of that world. But if we know that it exists, and is a cause, we do in fact know something about it. Why, then, should we not return to the philosophical claim that Kant had reluctantly abandoned, and posit that reason does tell us something positive about the intelligible world of things-in-themselves?

The German Idealists, perhaps the best known of whom are Schelling, Fichte and Hegel, argued that if reality is rational, and if human reason is able to understand the structure of reality, then our rational postulates will give us some information about the inner structure of being-in-itself. This will not be scientific knowledge (what Kant called theoretical knowledge), which is confined to the world of appearance. It will be based on the insight that in interpreting experience and seeking to explain it, in our confidence in mathematics as the key to understanding reality, and in our freedom to act on self-legislated principles, we are in practice committing ourselves to the rule of reason over the world of sensory experience. It is in our rational and moral agency that we may find that reason is not the slave of the passions, but a guide to directing our passions to intrinsically good ends, and a testimony to our own transcendence over all that belongs to the sensory world.

Perhaps we can agree with Kant that reality-in-itself is beyond our comprehension, and that we must never claim that it is exactly as we envisage it. But we may claim that our models for envisaging it are adequate to our intellectual and moral actions in this world, and to confirm our natural belief that reason and goodness will finally triumph in the world of human experience, as they rule in the hidden world that is the kingdom of the ultimately real.

Philosophical Idealism was the dominant force in European philosophy until the early twentieth century. It followed the major European tradition of taking human sensory experience as the starting-point of all knowledge, but then of distinguishing sensory experience, as a world of appearances, from knowledge of the essential nature of reality, which is rational mind or consciousness.

This tradition entered deeply into traditional Christian religion, for which the world of time is an appearance and sacrament of an eternal reality. But it was not confined to Christianity. For many philosophers, orthodox religion was too dogmatic, and contained too much superstition, legend and literalism about ancient texts, to be truly rational. Hume rejected religion as morally repressive and infantile, but it is noteworthy that he also enslaved reason to the passions. In trying to confine knowledge to experience alone, it is arguable that he undermined the foundations of both science and of his own philosophy. Kant also rejected religious claims to revelation and to personal experiences of God, which he found too often fantastical, prone to delusion, and irrational to be taken seriously. But Kant hoped for a 'moral religion', that would found moral striving on belief in God as the author of the moral law, and the guarantor of its final triumph in a world of evil and injustice.

The Idealist philosophers are not all friendly to the God of religion, or to what they perceive that God to be. Generally speaking, Absolute Idealists had little interest in the personal God of religion, whereas Personal Idealists identified that personal God with absolute Spirit. But they agree that the ultimate reality is mind or Spirit, in itself of supreme rationality and value, and the cause of everything in space and time. Some of them said that the material universe is not fully real, that it is an illusion, a confused appearance of reality. Others suggested that it is a positive expression of Spirit, playing a positive role in the self-manifestation of the nature of Spirit.

For Hegel, who will be more fully discussed in the next chapter, the existence of the space-time world enables Spirit to realise itself in new ways, and so to come to know itself in new ways, until all the potentialities of Spirit have been expressed, and all is taken back into the life of Spirit as a completed whole. The universe is the actualisation of Spirit, and Spirit is the completion of the universe, enfolded once more in the divine life.

This is metaphysics in the grand manner, expanded well beyond the limits Kant sought to put on it. But once Kant had distinguished reality and appearance, and assigned priority to mind, this development seems inevitable. In the end it is unsatisfactory to divide noumenal freedom and phenomenal determinism, necessity and contingency, reason and sensibility. Humans live in one world, of which reason, understanding and sensibility must together provide a coherent and plausible conceptual interpretation. This is the deepest implication of Kant's philosophy. For Kant was a metaphysical Idealist who affirmed God as the ground of the rationality of the real and the objectivity of morality, not the Kant of legend, the destroyer of both metaphysics and God.

Chapter 8

WHATEVER HAPPENED TO HEGEL?

At the end of the nineteenth century and the beginning of the twentieth Idealism was in the ascendant in philosophy. The Reformation and the Enlightenment encouraged people to be critical of ancient authorities and to think for themselves. One consequence was that philosophers began to think a thousand different things. Indeed, if a philosopher could not think of a new and original theory about the nature of reality, that philosopher was at once consigned to the second rank of disciples and lick-spittles. Originality was in the air, and every reputable philosopher had to have their own theory of reality.

Nevertheless, there were fairly clearly defined limits on possible philosophical theories. Some account had to be given of mind or consciousness and of its relation to the material universe. Was there one ultimate mind, or were there many, or was mind an illusion? Some view had to be taken on whether the whole system of being was necessary, or whether it was, even if only in part, contingent and free. Was individual personhood important, or was it only a small part of a wider whole? Did history have a purpose and goal, or was it a succession of pointless accidents?

These are all questions with which religions are also concerned. But philosophers may give answers which make religious practice pointless — as Nietzsche did. And philosophers in the Western tradition have mostly been concerned only with intellectual or speculative answers, and not with investigation of practices that seek to overcome selfish desire and achieve some sort of conscious relation to whatever ultimate reality is conceived to be. Moreover, philosophers often see religion as riddled with legends and myths, as expecting God or spirits to interfere constantly with natural processes, and as requiring submission to authority based on some holy text or weird emotional experience rather than on sound reason.

So philosophy after Kant in Germany became a set of diverse world-views with a very ambiguous relationship to any form of institutional religion. Nevertheless most of these views were spiritual in nature. That is, they saw ultimate reality as lying in a spiritual, non-material and conscious being or state. Among them, Georg Wilhelm Friedrich Hegel (1770–1831) was almost certainly the German philosopher who has been most influential on the history of thought.

Hegel's relation to religious thought has always been seen as ambiguous. On the one hand he was a Lutheran, and saw his mature philosophy as the first truly Christian metaphysical system. On the other, his early writings depict Christianity as an other-worldly and slavish religion, in contrast to the allegedly healthy-minded, fully social and democratic thought of ancient Greece. And when he came to accept Christianity, many suspect that it was because he had managed to reinterpret Christian faith in terms of his own philosophy rather than the other way around.

However that may be, although Hegel's philosophical writing is excessively complex and obscure, its main ideas are actually rather simple.[1] There is one ultimate reality, Spirit (*Geist*), and the whole history of the universe is the story of its gradual coming to full self-consciousness. In order to know itself, Spirit has to objectify itself, or regard itself as a series of objects of knowledge. These objects might be regarded as isolated, self-existing and contingently related elements, as they often are in science. But a deeper perception will show that no object is truly isolated or capable of existing alone. All objects imply their opposites, as light implies darkness or heat implies cold. To know things fully is to know things in their essential opposition to one another, an opposition that is implied by their very being, and that further implies a deeper unity within which the opposites are held together.

The universe is not a set of accidentally related and separate

Whatever Happened to Hegel?

elements. It is an organic unity, in which each part is related to the others in necessary ways. When this unity is fully realised, then Spirit has become fully conscious of itself, by reconciling the apparent diversity and alienation from Spirit of the objects of knowledge within one unitary consciousness. So the universe is the objective manifestation of Spirit, and it exhibits a historical process of development by which it is being reconciled to the life of Spirit – from which it has never in fact been separated, though it may have seemed to be – in a final conscious recognition and reconciliation of all opposites.

The Hegelian dialectic is the process through which Pure Being is alienated from itself by becoming what seems to be its polar opposite, brute matter. At each stage of the dialectic, a whole succession of opposites are gradually transcended in higher perceptions of underlying unity. The final stage of the dialectic is the unity of all things in the self-consciousness of Spirit, which has returned to itself from the alienated world which was always, in fact, the expression of the inner dynamics of its own being.

The root of Hegel's system is, as in all forms of idealism, that all objects are objects-for-consciousness, and that conscious selves are agents constructing intelligible understanding through active efforts of thought. Thus consciousness cannot be simply thought away, leaving objects existing, just as we conceive them, on their own. And purposive or goal-seeking agency is primarily known in intellectual enquiry, which presumes and confirms the intelligibility of the experienced world. Consciousness and purpose are primary both in our understanding of the world, and in objective reality itself. To deny them objective reality is to deny the very conditions of knowledge, and to mistake an imagined abstraction (a world of purely material particles or of self-existing mathematical formulae) for the concrete reality we know in our everyday conscious experience – though we have to use reason and understanding to discover its essential nature.

It has to be said that the Hegelian system has been almost wholly eradicated from the minds of many modern philosophers. I was never taught it at University. But then in my University philosophy course, virtually the whole of Continental European philosophy after Kant was a dark mystery, incapable of being translated into British thought or language. Perhaps its claim to provide a rigorous logical demonstration of the character of reality as Absolute Spirit was just too grandiose. The more technical and rigorous it tried to get, the more jargon-ridden and vacuous it seemed to many to be. And it was also implicated, rightly or wrongly, with subsequent forms of totalitarian thought, both in Communism and in German National Socialism.

This is partly because of Hegel's stress on the notion of organic unity, especially as applied to the State. Individual freedom, he held, is not some sort of personal choice made in independence of others. It is ideally the subordination of self to the community and its purposes. Individuals are parts of larger wholes, and must give themselves to playing a proper part in the self-manifestation of the *Volksgeist*, the spirit of the people. Unfortunately, the ground is laid here for the idea of a *Fuhrer*, an inspired individual who can define the spirit of the people, and enlist them in the great work of promoting the national consciousness.

This is rather unfair, since Hegel has in mind the whole global community as the manifestation of the self-realisation of Spirit. And that emerging global community has to be intelligible and rational, not dominated by false ideas of racial superiority and a desire for world domination, as Hitler's National Socialism was. But it has to be admitted that Hegel did seem to see Prussia as the place where Spirit was finally coming to fuller self-consciousness, so there was a sort of superiority in German culture and consciousness.

Moreover, there is an unhealthy emphasis in Hegel on the necessity of conflict and pain as part of the self-realisation of Spirit. If all things generate their contradictories through the dialectic of history, then evil becomes an essential part of good, and dialectic is all too easily equated with conflict. Perhaps in Hegel's identification of the events of history with a dialectical self-realisation of Spirit there is the danger of equating whatever happens with what ought to be. There is no objective reality of

Whatever Happened to Hegel?

pure goodness, apart from the world and judging it. How can there be, when all that happens in the world is a necessary realisation of Spirit itself?

That is part of the discomfort many Christians feel with Hegel. Absolute Spirit and the tragic events of human history are much too closely identified. Karl Marx saw that such an identification could be interpreted in another way, too. Instead of history being the self-realisation of Spirit, one could say that Spirit is just an emergent aspect of the processes of history. To speak of an 'objective God' is to invent a fantasy dissociated from the world. Whereas to speak of the dialectical process of history as inevitably culminating in a society of free conscious agents is to speak of the real struggles and possibilities of the world itself, not of some perfect being beyond the world, which might offer illusory compensation for the defects of life in the world.

Left-wing Hegelians drop all thought of a perfect all-determining reality beyond history, and interpret dialectical struggle and progress through conflict as referring to the one reality that ascends towards consciousness and freedom through its own inner dynamic, without guidance or interference from 'outside'. Marx claimed to have 'stood Hegel on his head'. But Hegelian Idealism is ambiguous enough to allow a Marxist type of interpretation, for which the idea of God is renounced, and attention is focused on the inner character of the universe itself. Since that inner character essentially involves conflict and the overcoming of the past by new forms of relationship, the way is paved for doctrines of perpetual revolution and conflict, and for the necessity of a rule of the strong, a 'dictatorship of the proletariat' that will eradicate old social forms and lead the way to a less individualistic and more holistic structure. Freedom is found in subservience to the State, and the Party becomes the ideal – thus ironically fulfilling Hegel's own prediction that all social conditions turn into their opposites, and the quest for total freedom becomes the oppressive rule of a State that knows and enforces what it sees to be good for individuals.

For these reasons Hegelian idealism is often seen as intrinsically opposed to liberalism, to the freedom of the individual and acceptance of a pluralistic society in which many diverse views can peaceably co-exist. Hegel is, according to Karl Popper, another enemy of the open society. It is only fair to point out, however, that Hegel did have a strong belief in individual freedom, and in the co-existence of diverse views (in fact they are essential to the dialectic of history). His concern was to counter very individualistic or even anarchical ideas of freedom, and to show that real freedom for individuals entails a complex society that makes a positive and worthwhile freedom, which opens up the possibility of doing many different things, possible. And pluralism is not just a contingent co-existence of opposed views. It is part of a historical process in which views learn from one another, even in their opposition, and in which wider and deeper understandings become possible.

We should remember, also, that Hegel did not seriously believe that history had come to an end with him, so that his philosophy was the final word. Hegelian idealism, too, must be just a stage on the journey of the self-understanding of Being. We should expect it to be superseded, even though it definitively expresses a number of new insights into the ultimate nature of reality.

What were these insights? One is the claim, radically new to Western philosophy, that the material universe is the progressive self-realisation of Spirit. Spirit is not something complete, perfect and unchanging, as it had been in Aristotle and Aquinas. Spirit essentially realises or objectifies itself in the material universe. We might even say that, for Hegel, Spirit is incomplete and unknown to itself until it does realise itself in an objective universe. So the universe becomes a necessary manifestation of Spirit, and Spirit is essentially changing and developing in and through the history of the universe.

Since this is the case, it follows that finite persons, including human beings, are not wholly distinct beings apart from God. They are parts of Absolute Spirit, transitory moments in the process of divine self-realisation. In a sense, humans are divine, or at least parts of the divine, and not miserable sinners cut off forever from God, unless God rather arbitrarily chooses to save them. Nevertheless, they may have a proper individuality and freedom. They may be able to help or impede the self-realisation of Spirit. Their destiny is to become conscious and voluntary vehicles of that Spirit as it moves towards its goal of full self-consciousness.

For classical theism, time and history made no difference to God. They did not change God in any way, and God would be the same whether or not any universe existed. But for Hegel, time and history change Spirit, and Spirit would not be what it is without them.

Furthermore, there is a development and progress in history. Evolution was a spiritual idea before it became a properly scientific one. It is the progress of the universe towards greater understanding of its nature as Spirit, and greater capacity to mediate the activity of Spirit in a more conscious way. Again, this is in sharp contrast with most traditional religious and philosophical views, which tend to see human history as a fall from a more perfect Golden Age, rather than a progress to a more golden future.

The evolutionary process moves forward through a dialectical process, in which opposition is the driving force towards higher and more inclusive forms of understanding. Matter seems to be the opposite of Spirit, in being unconscious, fragmented, diverse, and non-purposive. Yet it is the essential means by which Spirit becomes conscious of itself, as the material universe is integrated into the divine experience and made a progressively more transparent vehicle of the divine nature and purpose.

In a similar way, destruction seems the opposite of creation. Yet new forms of creativity only arise through the destruction of the old. Alienation and estrangement are paths to reconciliation and more comprehensive integration. In this Hegel saw a philosophical statement of the Christian principle that 'those who lose their life for my sake will find it' (Matt. 10:39). It is through self-renunciation, or through journeying into the far country, that we find and fulfil our true selves.

All the suffering and alienation of the world are thus parts of Spirit. It is no accident that Hegel was a Lutheran, inheriting the Lutheran 'theology of the cross', which stressed in a new way the suffering of God in and with the suffering of the world. The divine nature was no longer seen as immune from suffering, as wholly blissful and untouched by sorrow. Spirit embraces all the suffering of every world, though it transmutes (or 'sublates') it by placing it within a wider experience, wherein it can be used to realise new forms of goodness.

This is a remarkable reinterpretation of the philosophical idea of God. Though it is opposed to the classical Christian view of God at almost every point, it yet carries great resonance with many biblical perspectives. In the New Testament, humans are repeatedly said to live 'in Christ', and the disciples of Jesus are said to be 'parts of the body of Christ'. Since Christ is God, this does seem to entail that at least some, and possibly all, things are parts of God, in some sense.

Moreover, God weeps for Israel, Jesus weeps over Jerusalem, and a natural interpretation of Jesus' death is to say that here God is suffering with creation.

On the other hand, Christians have rarely felt that the creation of this universe is an essential part of God's own self-realisation, or that history will inevitably progress to a state of full universal self-consciousness. So Hegel's influence on Christian thought, while it has been profound, has often been disguised or even denied. Karl Barth, for instance, often writes as though he is free of all philosophical influences. But his view of God as changing, temporal, and suffering, is clearly influenced by Hegel. Teilhard de Chardin, writing in Hegelian fashion of human history moving towards an Omega point of planetary consciousness, was for a while forbidden to publish by the Roman Catholic authorities.

Yet it has become almost commonplace, especially in Protestant Christianity, to speak of God suffering with the world, and changing both in issuing divine initiatives and in responsive relationship to human acts. It has become common to speak of

God's action in the world as persuasive rather than pre-determining – acting within the processes of history rather than interfering with such processes. And post-Darwinian evolutionary biology has vindicated a generally evolutionary view of life – though scientific views rarely commit themselves to the postulate of a future goal of total self-consciousness towards which evolution moves.

One main strand of modern philosophy that could not have existed without German idealism is Whitehead's Process philosophy. Whitehead calls his system, another ambitious metaphysical world-view, the 'philosophy of organism', and this repeats the Hegelian stress on the universe as an organic unity, with all its parts constituting an organic whole, and contributing to an all-including cosmic consciousness.[2]

Whitehead recommends dropping the concept of 'substance' – one enduring and underlying nature that remains the same through all the changes of its properties. Instead he speaks of 'actual occasions' or 'events', which are chains of transitory point-instants in continual flux. The universe is a series of chains of events, and so it is in constant change.

Each event 'prehends', or internalises in its own being the immediately preceding events which causally influence it. Each event integrates such causal influences in a new and unique way, and projects into its immediate future a new set of causal influences arising from that integration.

Moreover, events are arranged in organic hierarchies. Subatomic events are included within larger systems to form atoms, then molecules, and then larger living organisms, and so on. So there is a hierarchy of organic systems, and the whole universe forms one organic system, within which all the past is prehended and integrated into one experience, and projected creatively into a new and open future.

'God' is the supremely inclusive reality, just like Hegel's Spirit. God's primordial being provides the possibilities for actual being, but it is in itself incomplete, since possibilities are not fully actual, and they need to be actualised. As in Hegel, some actual world is necessary if the nature of God is to be fully realised. But Whitehead differs from Hegel in placing causal priority not in the one Spirit, but in the many actual events that form an infinite series without beginning or end.

God does not unilaterally decide what is going to happen. In the series of events, each event prehends its immediate past and creatively projects its immediate future. Though there are many forms of co-ordination between events, and though they form organic wholes that influence the way they act, there is nevertheless no one determining Spirit that makes them act in a specific way. Whitehead's universe is essentially open and indeterminate, and cosmic history is the result of an infinite number of separate creative acts, which may well conflict with one another.

In this process there is an all-including divine experience, and in it all the experiences of all events are divinely prehended, sufferings and conflicts as well as enjoyments and creative collaborations. This is the consequential being of God, which integrates all finite experiences within itself. The existence of this consequential nature necessarily has a causal influence on the way things go in the universe. But it is precisely an influence, registered with different strengths and in different ways by each actual event, guiding the universe towards satisfactory outcomes, but always leaving the ultimate creative decisions to the infinite number of events which constitute its own being.

Whitehead stresses individual freedom and creativity more than Hegel, whose emphasis is rather on the self-realisation of the one supreme Spirit. But in both systems there is an inbuilt tendency towards the good, as Spirit seeks the most enriching and creative future for itself and for all its constitutive parts.

As is the case with Hegel, most Christian thinkers are wary of the grandiose metaphysical claims and what seem to be rather over-precise technical details of Process philosophy. But Christian thought – especially Protestant thought – has been deeply influenced by it. It is an attempt to work out what the universe must be like if consciousness and value (and the purposes that seek to realise value) are primary elements of reality, rather than unexpected and causally sterile side-effects of unconscious and directionless material forces. It takes evolutionary theory and post-relativity physics seriously. It insists that change and radical creativity are not imperfections, but positive values that must somehow be included in any idea of God as supreme perfection. It affirms that human history and development affect the being of God in important ways, so that the divine truly shares in the travails of creation. It affirms that humans are free to determine their own destinies, without being wholly determined by eternal divine decrees. And it sees the whole history of the cosmos as integrated forever in the consciousness of God, and so as contributing to a full realisation of consciously apprehended value that could in principle be shared by infinite numbers of different kinds of conscious beings.

Nineteenth-century idealism did bring about, at least for many, a transformation of the idea of that perfect self-existent reality that is God. Change and time, development and diversity, are made central or even essential to the idea of supreme value. Even if Spirit is capable of existing in that self-contemplating bliss of which Aristotle writes, there is distinctive value in the existence of a world of diverse spirits that can relate to one another in experience and action.

It may be necessary for Spirit to originate some such world, if it is to realise more completely its own possible perfections. It may even be necessary for Spirit, fully self-conscious and active, to generate its own opposite, a universe of matter, unconscious and inert, in order that within that world finite spirits should gradually emerge. From primitive and quasi-automatic responses to external stimuli, simple material beings develop complex and integrated structures, with forms of consciousness that can be fully sensitive and appreciative, and forms of active response that can be unique, co-operative and creative. Yet in such a universe there will necessarily be possibilities of conflict, as conscious spirits seek their own pleasure rather than the objectively good, and seek to consume and destroy rather than to co-operate and create.

Such a worldview provides a good reason why a finite universe should exist – for the realisation of values potential in the being of Spirit – whereas for Aristotle it might have been better for Spirit simply to exist on its own. It also provides an explanation for the existence of suffering – it, or at the very least its possibility, is essential to the diverse, developing, and interconnected nature of an emergent universe within which beings of largely self-determining consciousness and purpose originate. Such beings can conflict as well as co-operate, and they can choose personal good as well as the common good. It is not that suffering is a necessary means to good, but that suffering is a necessary consequence of a world in which goodness is to be attained by learning and striving.

Spirit, having originated such a world, will experience both the values and disvalues that the world generates, but its purpose will be to achieve a final integration and reconciliation of all these new and distinctive values, with the ending or transformation of all conflict and sorrow. The final integration will be the actualisation of a community of spirits who, having emerged through conflict and striving, can participate in the divine experience of the completed and transformed consciousness of the history of the universe. That history will at last truly be seen as the realisation of potentialities necessarily inherent in the divine Spirit.

This, I think, is a spiritual philosophy that builds on the classical traditions of Plato and Aristotle, but radically reformulates them in the light of that greater interest in science, in history, in evolution, and in the values of humanism, that characterised Europe after the sixteenth century. Whether it is, as Hegel claimed, a specifically Christian philosophy is a moot point. But perhaps it is not further removed from the teachings of Jesus than were the Platonically-influenced thoughts of the Church Fathers. Perhaps it offers a general philosophical perspective that could be appropriated by a number of religious traditions. Yet perhaps Hegel is right in thinking that the Christian teachings of self-giving as the path to a new resurrected life in God, of the kingdom of God as a reconciled community of love, and of God as entering into time and suffering in order that finite beings could be enabled to participate in the life of God, have a very close affinity with the main teachings of post-nineteenth-century idealism. Philosophy and religion remain distinct. But each may illuminate the other in a significant way. If they do, both may be the better for it. To have a reflectively informed religion and a spiritually sensitive philosophy is not a bad aim for anyone who wishes to understand the human condition in all its ambiguity and complexity.

WHY SCHOPENHAUER WAS NOT QUITE AN ATHEIST

The main Western philosophical tradition has placed a supreme
spiritual reality firmly at the centre of reflective thinking about
human life and knowledge. But there has always been a counter-
tradition. It would be silly to say that there have not been atheists
in every generation. I am not saying that. All I am saying is that
belief in God has been considered the most rational foundation of
a thoughtful view of human existence by most classical philosophers throughout Western history. Moreover, when belief in
God is consciously and thoroughly overthrown, belief in reason,
in morality, and in the significance of human existence, also tends
to disappear. I will illustrate this by reference to two major
atheistic philosophers of the nineteenth century. Thus I hope to
show how the elimination of belief in God has led, historically,
to the overthrow of the basic philosophical and scientific faith
that the universe is intelligible and that reason is a trustworthy
guide to understanding it. Far from being irrational, belief in God
is the safeguard of the rational structure of the cosmos, and of the
importance of reason in understanding human existence.

David Hume foreshadowed the demise of reason in his radically empirical philosophy, though his remaining Scottish common sense saved him from fully accepting the conclusions of his
own philosophy. Hume was an exception in his own day, and
was not then as highly regarded as the theistic 'common-sense'
philosophers of the Scottish Enlightenment. But it is arguable
that things began to change in the late eighteenth and the
nineteenth centuries.

Philosophers have always been an independent-minded bunch. Plato and Aristotle did not see themselves as having much in common with the religious pantheons of ancient Athens. Spinoza was excommunicated from the synagogue in Amsterdam. Immanuel Kant never attended a church, even when it was thought to be his duty to do so.

One reason for this is that philosophers usually try to reflect on human life without appealing to revelation, miracles, or religious authorities. They may not place 'reason' very highly in their schemes – Hume certainly did not – but they do value independence of thought, and tend to be wary of just accepting dogmas without question.

When the authority of the Catholic Church in Europe was radically weakened by the Protestant Reformation, which coincided with the invention of printing, the opportunity to express such independence of thought was hugely increased. As various competing systems of philosophy sprang up, and as scientific knowledge of the natural world increased, it became rarer to find major philosophers subordinating their views to the authority of a church, as Aquinas had done.

Indeed, to propound a unique and new philosophy became a virtue or even a professional obligation for anyone who aspired to be a major philosopher. It was slightly odd that each new philosophical worldview claimed to be the final truth, hidden from all previous philosophers, when what was valued was precisely the novelty and imaginative richness of each new philosophy. And it was odd for philosophers to claim that their own systems, arrived at simply by sitting and thinking, could provide the true and hidden meaning of all ancient religious traditions, with their centuries of spiritual discipline and innumerable saints and savants, and show that religions were fumbling or inept attempts to find the true philosophy that they (but not, of course, their closest colleagues) had at last discerned. But so it was.

'No one who is a philosopher is in a true sense religious. He walks free of the leash, precariously but free',[1] writes my first witness, Arthur Schopenhauer (1788–1860), propagating the self-deluding myth that philosophers are free spirits, unencumbered by tradition and culture, whereas the religious are passively obedient to authority. Schopenhauer is sometimes called the archetypal 'philosopher of pessimism', and Nietzsche described him as the first German philosophical atheist. Schopenhauer, however, was not an atheist in any straightforward sense. He was, and claimed to be, a transcendental idealist in the tradition of Kant. That is, he began from a study of human consciousness, and from an acceptance that sense-experience gives knowledge only of a world of appearances, not of things as they are in themselves. There is a hidden reality, but scientific or descriptive forms of knowledge give no access to it. We can know that it must exist (appearances must be appearances of something), but theoretical knowledge of it is impossible.

In Kant's case, there are 'practical', morally based, postulates – God, freedom, and immortality – that legislate how we must think of reality-in-itself, though we must deny them theoretical adequacy. In the previous chapter, I showed how Hegel ditched this Kantian agnosticism, and restored Kant's earlier belief that reason could give a true account of objective reality. In the course of doing so, Hegel formulated a new idea of Absolute Spirit (*Geist*) as realising itself in a progressive and dialectical fashion in time and history. For Hegel, reality was thoroughly rational (reason, for him, remember, was a dynamic, creative and imaginative faculty), and history was a progressive movement towards full understanding, and a truly good, happy and fulfilled society. Thus God (absolute Spirit) is fundamentally rational, good, purposive and concerned to bring about human happiness and fulfilment.

Already in Hegel, however, there are the seeds of a rather different outlook. Absolute Spirit, after all, does not seem to be a fully personal God who answers prayers and performs miraculous acts to save various unlikely groups of people. Spirit may be just the dialectical process of history, and that process, far from being kindly and benevolent, involves suffering and conflict in an essential way. Prayer understood as communication with a supernatural personal being, miracles as the specific unique acts of such a being, revelation as the authoritative disclosure of that being, and consequently the authority of churches and religious institutions, take a secondary role. The philosopher, the discerner of the patterns of the historical process, replaces the saint, rapt in contemplation of the Eternal but achieving nothing of historical value.

It was this more negative side of Hegel that marked the thought of Schopenhauer. But he went much further than Hegel had done. Whereas Hegel had seen suffering as necessary to a fundamentally good process, Schopenhauer saw existence itself as essentially suffering. The most basic reason for his rejection of God was that no benevolent God could create such a world of intense suffering. There is an underlying reality, and it may be described as spiritual. But it is not good or rational. What then is it?

'Every glance at the world, to explain which is the task of the philosopher, confirms and establishes the will-to-live ... the only true description of the world's innermost nature.'[2] Schopenhauer replaces Hegel's Reason by Will, the ceaseless striving for being, for 'life, and then to the highest possible degree thereof'.

'The whole world, like man himself, is through and through will and through and through representation, and beyond this there is nothing.'[3] The world is a representation to consciousness (that is transcendental idealism), but it is also 'will', the ruthless, incessant, relentless striving for life. 'What is the thing-in-itself? Our answer has been the will',[4] he writes.

Will is not beneficent, for the darkest truth is that being is in the end not desirable. 'This world itself', he says, 'is the worst of all possible worlds.'[5] It gives rise to endless suffering, and Christianity is rejected by Schopenhauer because it seeks to disguise this fact, and pretend that all is good and in order. Indeed, 'Our existence is happiest when we perceive it least; from this it follows that it would be better not to have it.'[6]

It has to be admitted that this is pessimism. It is hard to turn the belief that it would be better not to exist in this, the worst of all possible worlds, into a hidden declaration of optimism. And yet ... even the most gloomy of philosophers does not write large volumes just to state that life is miserable. Like Spinoza, Schopenhauer believes that 'salvation' from misery is possible, even if only for a few souls. 'There is a spiritual world', he writes in his early notebooks, 'and in it we are separated from all the phenomena of the external world.'[7]

We know that we only see the world as appearance, phenomenon. And we know that there is a reality-in-itself beyond all phenomena. It may seem, from what has been said, that this reality is 'will'. But that is not so clear (nothing is in Schopenhauer). He writes, 'The thing-in-itself, which we know most immediately in the will, may have ... modes of existence ... which then remain as the inner nature of the thing-in-itself, when this ... has freely abolished itself as will.'[8]

It seems that reality may not be just sheer will-to-live, though that is how it expresses itself in the time of our experienced world. It may also include the denial of the will-to-live, in its being beyond all phenomena, which of course does not appear phenomenally. Surprisingly, however, we can in some sense have access to this aspect of reality. Because 'our own inner being nevertheless belongs of necessity to the world of things-in-themselves ... it must yet be possible to lay hold of some data for explaining the connection between the world of phenomena and the being-in-itself of things. Here, therefore, lies the path on which I have gone beyond Kant and the limit he set.'[9] In some way humans can intuit or have some form of apprehension of the inner nature of reality beyond its self-expressive willing.

When we look inwards, and away from the world of phenomena, there is a sort of non-conceptual awareness of a final denial of the will to express being phenomenally, and that he calls 'salvation from the world'. In fact, he writes, 'that great fundamental truth contained in Christianity as well as in Brahmanism and Buddhism, the need for salvation from an existence given up to suffering and death, and its attainability through the denial of the will ... is beyond all comparison the most important truth there can be.'[10]

He seems to speak positively here of Christianity. But he believes that 'Christianity has recently forgotten its true significance, and has degenerated into shallow optimism.'[11] 'Religion is the metaphysics of the people ... an allegorical way of expressing the truth.'[12] But religion is also wreathed in legends and false or unverifiable historical claims, and in particular it overlays the truth of salvation through the denial of the will with all sorts of dogmatic affirmations about a loving personal God.

There are 'two inseparable qualities of God, namely personality and causality'.[13] The postulation of such a being is childish and impossible, since these are necessarily qualities only of phenomenal reality, and belief in their objective, transcendental, existence can only serve to trap one in the coils of suffering and death, since they still express attachment to the will-to-live.

'The better consciousness in me', he says, 'lifts me into a world where there is no longer personality and causality or subject and object ... for that reason I hope that it is no God. But if anyone wants to use the expression God symbolically for that better consciousness itself ... so let it be, yet not among philosophers I should have thought.'[14]

This 'better consciousness' lifts one to a realm beyond all finite representations. 'This consciousness lies beyond all experience and thus beyond all reason.'[15] At this point we might easily feel that we have indeed moved beyond all reason. We have a thing-in-itself which is beyond all knowledge and description, and yet our 'inner consciousness' (which must surely be phenomenal) somehow provides awareness of its innermost character. We have consciousness which is not experience. And we have knowledge which communicates nothing (though only a 'relative nothing', he says).

To put it charitably, we could say that Schopenhauer is here struggling to express the inexpressible. And he is placing a question mark against the ability of reason to encompass the nature of things: 'The intellect is, so to speak, a mere superficial force ... and does not penetrate into the very essence of things.'[16]

There is much in theistic traditions, of course, to support the view that God is ultimately beyond understanding or ineffable in the divine essence. As Baron von Hügel said, any God who could be wholly understood by humans would hardly be worthy of the name. But that is perfectly compatible with saying that there is much about God that can be understood, especially with regard to God's relation to the world as creator and redeemer.

It is when Schopenhauer denies that anything can be known about the thing-in-itself, and then proceeds to speak of direct knowledge of it, that things get difficult. 'That state which is experienced by all who have attained to complete denial of the will ... cannot really be called knowledge, since it no longer has the form of subject and object; moreover it is accessible only to one's own experience that cannot be further communicated.'[17]

The problem is that Schopenhauer is communicating it quite well and in two lengthy volumes. He may mean that we cannot say what it 'feels like', but then that is true of looking at a beautiful view too. The best we can do is to say that it is some sort of consciousness where the distinction between subject and object has been lost, and one is not aware of space and time. But then how do we know that it is describable as 'denial of the will', and that it is genuine consciousness of the inner nature of reality-in-itself, rather than just being a particularly odd sort of phenomenal experience?

What Schopenhauer tends to do is to concentrate on different sorts of human consciousness. On the one hand, there is attachment to the pleasure of life, which leads to suffering and death. On the other hand, there is 'the quieter of every willing ... the state of voluntary renunciation, resignation, true composure, and complete will-lessness'.[18] This is 'a peace that is higher than all reason. That ocean-like calmness of the spirit, that deep tranquillity, that unshakeable calmness and serenity ... only knowledge remains, the will has vanished'.[19]

Why should this be taken as more than a description of two

states of human consciousness, one apparently life-affirming yet in fact leading to suffering and unhappiness, the other apparently life-denying yet leading to liberation from suffering and deep tranquillity?

This is a problem that was to cast its shadow over later so-called 'Existentialist' philosophers like Sartre and Heidegger, who are the heirs of Schopenhauer's approach to philosophy. They speak primarily of the human way of being in the world. They speak of the inauthentic lives of the mass of humanity, who fail to perceive the real nature of the human condition. They speak of the importance of living authentically, in full acceptance of radical human freedom, in full awareness of the finitude of human existence, and of the need to create meaning for oneself in a world without a personal God who could lay down rational and moral standards and give an objective purpose to existence.

But are they in fact doing any more than express personal and subjective attitudes to human experience? If there is no such thing as absolute truth, attainable by human reason or experience, why should their views be accepted as universally true? Are they not just expressing the perspective of one particular subculture, or of their own personal outlook on life? If one wants to live inauthentically, or to live one's life by playing out a series of roles (even if others choose to see that as 'bad faith'), and if one does not care for denial of the will, or for a life of deep tranquillity, or freedom from convention, or the calm acceptance of death, why should one pay any attention to these seemingly ceaselessly introspective philosopher-poets?

The fact is that they see themselves as possessing and conveying an insight into the nature of reality that makes certain attitudes more appropriate or 'authentic' than others. Schopenhauer is not just recommending denial of the will as a practical way of avoiding suffering. There is a meaning to human life that is not just arbitrarily invented. There is a 'properly human way to live', and if this is paradoxically described as 'inventing your own meaning', then that testifies to the radical freedom and creativity in which the meaning of human life lies. It is not a meaning arbitrarily laid down by some personal God. But it is written into the nature of things, and humans find fulfilment by discovering and expressing it in their lives.

So Schopenhauer holds that the 'will to live' is an objective character of all phenomenal reality. But it is also what he calls the 'original guilt' of human consciousness, an orientation that inevitably leads to disappointment and suffering, and that can never attain final satisfaction. There is a way to the ending of suffering. Denial of the will, of attachment and striving, gives access to a deeper level of reality, beyond subject–object thinking, the nearest thing of all to a 'knowledge without will', a union with the character of reality beyond that which is expressed in the phenomenal world.

This aspect of the inner hidden unity of all things is very important to Schopenhauer. Beyond phenomena, reality must be one and undivided. The same reality that expresses itself in the division and disunity of the phenomenal world also remains in itself one and undivided, tranquil and serene. We humans can sense that unity as well as the dynamic multiplicity of 'the world'. If and when we do so, we shall find that a certain sort of moral commitment follows from our insight into the inner character of reality.

Schopenhauer is very clear that denial of the will is not just a matter of subjective preference that may appeal mainly to timid or pessimistic souls. It connects us to the heart of reality itself, and that heart is not a heart of sheer indifference, but of universal compassion, sympathy, or pity (*Mitleid* – the German word can bear each translation, but 'compassion' is most often used in translations of Schopenhauer).

It turns out that reality has objective moral significance after all – 'That the world has only a physical and not a moral significance is a fundamental error, one that is the greatest and most pernicious, the real perversity of mind.'[20]

Schopenhauer may have learned the importance of morality from Kant, but he came to reject the Kantian approach to morality. 'Kant's practical reason and categorical imperative are wholly unjustified, groundless and fictitious assumptions.'[21] There are only three basic motivations for human conduct, and they are egoism, malice and compassion. Kant, he thinks, did not move beyond a long-term egoism, in his postulate of happiness-in-accordance-with-virtue. Compassion is the only genuine moral incentive, and compassion is not a disposition that one decides to adopt. It springs from 'the intuitive knowledge that recognizes in another's individuality the same inner nature as in one's own'.[22]

That is to say, when one 'sees', or experiences in a non-conceptual way, that there is only one ultimate reality, of which, in one's own inner nature, one is part, then the difference between self and not-self disappears. The feelings of another are also one's own, and so the awareness of suffering and the possibility of release give rise to compassion for all beings who are lost in 'the world', but can achieve salvation and a 'peace higher than reason' if they can attain the great renunciation.

It is no surprise to learn that Schopenhauer read the *Upanishads* every day, and his philosophy does seem to be a Western version of a form of non-theistic Hinduism that is closely akin to Buddhism. He is an atheist in that he denies a personal and finite God. But he does believe that there is a supra-sensory reality whose nature is peace and compassion, which can be accessed by human minds, and which is the basis of the only truly moral incentive and of salvation from the suffering and attachments of the world.

This is not pessimism or atheism in any straightforward sense. Reality is essentially spiritual or beyond the physical, and humans can find release from suffering by attaining knowledge of it. Schopenhauer has not entirely left the classical Western perspective of a supreme spiritual good of which the world is an appearance. But he does remove some major elements of philosophical theism.

In trying to make some assessment of Schopenhauer's philosophy, it is first of all clear that his belief that this is the worst of all possible worlds is at odds with traditional theistic belief that the universe is both intelligible and beautiful, and that it contains many states of great value. The strong sense of alienation, of the unsatisfactoriness of existence in a universe without goal or purpose, is akin to the perception in most religions that human existence without God is indeed ultimately without significance. But it is hard not to feel that the inherent evil of existence is over-emphasised by Schopenhauer. There is some reason to think that human existence does not just express a blind will-to-live, purposeless striving, ruthless competition, and amoral driving energy. That is perhaps a description of life without God, without objective value and purpose. But there is more to be said for the goodness of life than Schopenhauer allows.

There is, he holds, salvation from the world. But such salvation lies in the cessation of personality (subject and object no longer exist), and of creative willing, and there is no sense to be made of the idea of the salvation *of* the world, or of its existence in a transformed and renewed state. While the spiritual value of non-attachment and of a tranquil consciousness is affirmed, it does not seem justifiable, on his own terms, to say that the experience of a 'peace higher than reason' gives adequate knowledge of the nature of reality-in-itself. That may be one form of an ego-transcending union with a higher spiritual reality. But Schopenhauer's transcendental idealism should forbid him from claiming that it tells one what the ultimate spiritual reality actually is.

In the Upanishadic traditions that he values, another form of spiritual experience, notably different from that of oceanic peace or inactivity, is the experience of joy in the good things of the world, but without attachment to them, and the creativity or 'play' (*lila*) of life in conscious relation to the Supreme Lord (*Isvara*), who is the personal form of ultimately ineffable reality. It is strange that this spiritual insight should be excluded by Schopenhauer. Perhaps it is because he rejects the idea of a monarchical, anthropomorphic, tyrannical, repressive God. But God does not have to be conceived in that way. There can be a serving, loving, luring and co-operating Lord, who is the personal and accessible aspect of a reality that is also beyond subject and object, beyond human comprehension in its totality. Indeed, it seems more reasonable to see the phenomenal expression of the Real as having some sort of positive function, rather than as a regrettable 'overflow' of transcendent being.

There is also a problem with Schopenhauer's idea of salvation as complete will-denial, in that very few individuals will ever attain to it. Salvation is for a tiny elite, and is not by any means a universal possibility. Hindus and Buddhists resolve that problem by allowing many, indeed innumerable rebirths, although that may be depressing in its own way. But it seems that the tiny gleam of optimism that Schopenhauer allows will pass almost everyone by. What is lacking here is some idea of grace and forgiveness, by which a more personal ground of being might manage to provide all beings with the possibility of continued growth towards salvation, despite their weaknesses and failures.

This connects with a final point, Schopenhauer's description of ultimate reality as compassionate. He holds that true morality is grounded in compassion, which arises from the realisation in experience that all beings are ultimately one, and that their apparently individual willing, striving and effort must cease. Such a morality has no positive goals that could be achieved by worldly existence, and it does not value relationship, friendship and love as important intrinsic goods. Genuine compassion, however, should issue in appropriate action, and that might lead one to expect that the ultimately real will be active in aiding finite beings in their misery, rather than impassive. In other words, it will be more like an agent than like an impersonal state – an insight which transformed many varieties of Buddhism, especially in the *Mahayana* traditions, from being solely a striving to blow out the fires of desire, to including a more recognisably religious set of practices of devotion to *Bodhisattvas*, compassionate beings who help their devotees. When such notions of devotion to spiritual beings who actively help their devotees appear, we are not after all so very far from the idea of an actively compassionate God.

Schopenhauer's philosophy does reject some major elements of theistic philosophy, but it retains a spiritual view that can be recognised as part, though it has to be said a very one-sided and negative part, of classical notions of God as infinitely beyond finitude and comprehension. It is a sort of pared-down spirituality, which in its zeal to reject inadequate and simplistic notions of God begins to gnaw at the roots of theism, though not at the ideas of morality, salvation and spirituality. In Schopenhauer the Western spiritual tradition retains its force, though tempered by reaction against naïve and anthropocentric ideas of God and against the over-optimistic dreams of an idealistic philosophy which tended to see human history as a progress towards a future perfect state that might look rather like an improved nineteenth-century Prussia.

It was Friedrich Nietzsche who pushed these thoughts to their extreme conclusion, dispensing with reason, morality and meaning, and proclaiming that God was not even a symbolic term for an ineffable reality beyond will and representation. God was finally and completely dead. Whether this is a liberating or a horrifying prospect remains to be seen.

Chapter 10

WAS NIETZSCHE A BAD THING?

Friedrich Nietzsche (1844–1900) set himself to overturn the whole Western tradition in philosophy. At first influenced by Schopenhauer, he went on to reject the views of 'the prophet of the great weariness', as he described him, and to develop his own very different philosophy. I say 'philosophy', but it is doubtful whether Nietzsche is a philosopher at all in the traditional sense. He is a poet and aphorist, the declaimer of a new 'Dionysian' way of life, but he has no patience with abstract metaphysical arguments, and, like Hume and Schopenhauer, he does not rate reason very highly. 'The irrationality of a thing is no argument against its existence, rather a condition of it', he says.[1] 'With all things one thing is impossible – rationality.'[2]

There is going to be no place in Nietzsche for explorations of what it might mean for the universe to be completely rational, or of what the nature of a perfectly rational and perfect being (God) might be. The universe is just there, a brute series of facts without meaning, purpose, reason or moral basis. Influenced by Schopenhauer's notion of the universe as the expression of a blind will-to-be, Nietzsche rejected what he regarded as a betrayal of this insight – namely, Schopenhauer's view that there was nevertheless a spiritual and compassionate reality underlying the phenomenally expressed will.

There is no such reality – 'God is dead', the prophet Zarathustra proclaims. That means there is no spiritual reality, and no objective morality either. 'There are no moral facts whatever. Moral judgement has this in common with religious judgement, that it believes in realities which do not exist.'[3]

Nietzsche clearly perceives the relation between asserting the existence of a rational God and asserting the existence of an objective morality (which would be based upon the rationally formed purposes of such a God). He sees the relation, and reacts to it with loathing and revulsion. 'Sick, miserable, filled with ill-will towards himself; full of hatred for the impulses towards life, full of suspicion of all that was still strong and happy. In short, a "Christian".'[4]

If there were a God who had purposes that humans just had to accept and conform to, this would breed servility systematically into human nature. 'The idea of a God is disturbing and humiliating.'[5] It would mean that someone was watching everything you did, and judging it, holding you accountable for what you did, and probably finding that it was insufficient and wrong, and punishing you for it. 'For youthful vigorous barbarians Christianity is poison; to implant the teaching of sinfulness and damnation into the heroic, childish and animal soul of the ancient German, for example, is nothing other than to poison it.'[6]

The sick soul hates itself, hates life, hates strength, heroism, and happiness, because it longs for another (wholly imaginary) life and condemns courage and pride and freedom and the love of this life. Nietzsche presumably knew whereof he spoke. His father and both grandfathers were Lutheran ministers. They had, one must suppose, preached of humans as miserable worms bowed down by their own sinfulness, whose only hope was blindly to obey the laws laid down by God, and dream of finding a deferred happiness in a life after death which they might obtain, if they entirely negated their will-to-live, and if God decided, of his inscrutable and inexorable will, to overlook their corrupted human natures.

Against all this, Nietzsche proclaims: 'I entreat you, my brothers, remain true to the earth, and do not believe those who speak to you of superterrestrial hopes! They are poisoners ... they are despisers of life.'[7] In his mind, Christians despise life, and therefore they despise themselves. What is needed is to be 'true to the earth', to affirm the goodness of the body, of the material world, and of material pleasure.

Was Nietzsche a Bad Thing?

This is partly because he believed that Kant had destroyed all arguments for God, and that there were no good reasons for believing that God exists. But it was more importantly because he rejected the Kantian postulates of God and immortality as evasions of the fact of the suffering of the world, which Schopenhauer had so effectively exposed. 'The world seemed to me the work of a suffering and tormented God.'[8] Only an imperfect or sadistic God could create a world of such suffering, and take delight in it. To think that such a sadistic and tormented God was some sort of moral paradigm would be perverse.

Not only so, but to look for happiness only in an 'afterworld' is to devalue this world, and to adopt an 'evil and misanthropic' attitude.[9] 'The enlightened man says: I am body entirely, and nothing beside.'[10] There can be no life beyond the body, and the idea of 'spiritual pleasures' is a fantasy. Those who love themselves will love the body, its health, strength and happiness. Contemplation and prayer are useless diversions, when the body calls for action and struggle.

Moreover, worship of an imagined God is a form of obsequiousness that demeans free human beings. Already in Kant there was an expressed dislike of prayer, as an unbecoming self-humiliation and servile cringing before God. Human autonomy did not allow obedience to a set of alleged divine commands set down in some holy book. Nietzsche accepts this thought, and presses it to its conclusion. A truly human being will not bow to any superior authority. A free person will have no 'devout spittle-licking and fawning before the God of Hosts',[11] but will insist upon being the author of its own way of life and moral principles, by its sheer willing.

These are basically not metaphysical but moral arguments, about the distastefulness of subordinating one's will to another ('It is a disgrace to pray'),[12] and about the nobility of making your own creative will the measure of all things. 'We certainly do not want to enter into the kingdom of heaven', he writes; 'we have become men, so we want the kingdom of earth'.[13] We do not want to be ruled by another, who tells us what is right and wrong and demands that we simply obey. We want to rule ourselves, to decide what is right and wrong, and thereby to become fully mature.

There are, however, some notable paradoxes in Nietzsche's view. The greatest paradox is the call to become radically free in a universe that is apparently ruled by chance, blind fate, and necessity. 'The theory of freedom of will is an invention of ruling classes', he writes.[14] He elaborates on this: 'The history of the moral sensations is the history of an error, the error of accountability, which rests on the error of freedom of will ... No one is accountable for his deeds.'[15] The true philosopher must affirm 'the unconditional unfreedom and unaccountability of the will'.[16]

If freedom of the will is 'an error', and if no one can help what they do, if we are helpless in the grip of nature, then does it make sense to preach that absolute freedom and autonomy is the destiny of humanity? For Kant this paradox was 'resolved' by making a huge distinction between the phenomenal and noumenal worlds, and saying that we could be free in the noumenal world, while being determined in the phenomenal. This almost wholly implausible suggestion is not open to Nietzsche, who has ruthlessly eradicated the noumenal world, and left only the world as it appears to consciousness (though at least he had not, like some of his successors, eradicated consciousness).

Freedom is either an error or it is not. But we cannot say that it is an error, and then call upon everyone to be free! It would be consistent to say that we cannot help what we do, think, or feel (as some Lutheran preachers did). But if so, to be wholly determined by God is no worse than being wholly determined by irrational and blind forces of nature. And if we are so determined, why not admit the fact, and carry on grovelling to God – since we will do so if we have been thus predetermined, anyway. There can hardly be any coherent protest against such behaviour, for which we should not be held accountable (incidentally, neither should God, since God is presumably determined by his own inscrutable nature too).

On the other hand, if we are free to decide how to think and act, then such freedom is a very important objective fact about the world. And that fact seems to give rise to at least one moral imperative, which will also be objective, or rooted in objectivity: 'Be free!' Is this not Zarathustra's insight into the nature of human existence in the world that leads him to go down to the world of humanity and preach his doctrine?

Then, of course, we find that the Zarathustrian doctrine does not only consist in the one near-vacuous exhortation: 'Be free!' Freedom has to be used in a particular way. To be free is to choose *not* to obey the words of any God or the conventions of 'the common herd'. It is to choose *not* to pine for a kingdom of heaven, or for a 'peace beyond reason' and beyond the earth. It is to affirm the earth, to 'live dangerously', to be courageous, bold and creative. 'Have I been understood?' asks Nietzsche in *Dionysus against the Crucified*.[17] In other words – do not choose to follow the way of self-immolation and penance. Rather follow the way of abundant life and joy and self-affirmation.

'Morality is nothing other (therefore no more) than obedience to customs ... The free human being is immoral because in all things he is determined to depend upon himself.'[18] The free person must act beyond good and evil, and not conform to morality or custom. That is a pretty clear recommendation.

It is indeed a paradoxical situation for a prophet to say that you must act on no authority, but decide everything for yourself – and then to tell you how to act and live. Or is Zarathustra saying no more than: 'This is how I have chosen to live. You can do that if you choose'? Surely the prophet is exposing the false consciousness of Christians, those 'cross-spiders' and lick-spittles, and revealing what it is to be truly human, to be, as he variously describes it, 'German', 'pagan', a 'blond beast', a yea-sayer, a Dionysian.

Why, after all, should one not choose to be a reasonably contented member of the herd, to find pleasure in worshipping a superior being, and to feel pity for the sorrows of the world? Would Zarathustra not feel contempt for such a one? And yet that is how they may choose to exercise their freedom.

Zarathustra is claiming to give a specific insight into the world of human existence, an insight that generates a specific way-of-being-in-the-world, a set of evaluations and attitudes that rules out other goals and purposes (for instance, religious and world-denying ones) as founded on error or timidity and cowardice. The most basic of these recommended attitudes is the will-to-life – interestingly, the opposite of Schopenhauer's teaching (which must throw doubt on any claim that there is just one non-religious attitude that is opposed to just one religious attitude – things are much more diverse than that).

'To redeem the past and to transform every "It was" into an "I wanted it thus!" – that alone do I call redemption!'[19] The use of the word 'redemption' here points to the author's concern with finding some practical and effective solution to life's main problem: how to live well and appropriately as a human being. There is a problem: most people do not live well. There is a diagnosis: people cannot face up to the truth about their situation in a universe without God, objective morality or purpose or meaning. There is a solution: Make everything that happens to you into something that you could have positively willed, and that you could will again and again.

One who truly affirms life will say: 'Was that life? Well then! Once more!'[20] For if you have joy in life, 'Joy wants itself, wants eternity, wants recurrence', and says, 'Yes to all woe as well.'[21] This is the doctrine of eternal recurrence, perhaps more of a moral assertion than a serious factual one. It is not that we are fated to live our lives, exactly as they are, an infinite number of times. It is rather that we should so affirm our lives, with all their suffering as well as with all their happiness, that we can gladly endure the thought of re-living them an infinite number of times.

If eternal recurrence is a factual hypothesis, it is more unlikely than most religious assertions about the existence of further lives, and if it is a moral hypothesis, it expresses heroism more extreme than most religions could stomach. If we find Schopenhauer's pessimism too extreme, many of us would find the thought that we should have exactly the same experiences over and over again without end quite unacceptable. It is possible to feel that there are many very good things in life, even that overall our lives are worth living, without wanting to re-live them without end. We might think of some improvements that would be nice, so why should we have to affirm the bad things as well as the good?

It may even seem a morally perverse attitude to say that we should affirm either our own suffering or that of others. This perversity appears most strongly when Nietzsche inveighs against 'pity' or 'compassion' (*Mitleid*) as weakness. 'What in the world has caused more suffering than the follies of the compassionate?' he asks.[22] 'Be warned against pity ... all great love is above pity.' Whereas Schopenhauer had taught that there are three great motives for action: egoism, malice and pity, Nietzsche rejects all motives except egoism. Those who claim to be motivated by altruism are deceiving themselves. They are really only motivated by the pleasure that altruistic action might bring to them. So Nietzsche teaches that we should embrace egoism, bring it out in the open, and, if we give to others, do so because in that way we show our munificence, out of the excess of the affirmation of our own will, not out of a pretended suffering-with-others. 'The noble human being, too, aids the unfortunate but not, or almost not, from pity, but more from an urge begotten by superfluity of power.'[23]

Sympathetic suffering can only add to the amount of suffering in the universe. It is in itself useless, and it is dishonest about real human motivations. For Schopenhauer, compassion naturally arises when one senses a unity with the desireless denial of the will that characterises the thing-in-itself, the ultimately real in its quiescence. For Nietzsche, there is no such ultimately real. The individual is never absorbed into the One. Each individual expresses a will-to-power that inevitably competes with all other individuals, and perpetually seeks its own self-aggrandisement.

Thus there is a specific assessment of human nature in Nietzsche, an assessment that sees all human conduct as egoistic, competitive, and always unsatisfied – 'the will to power, the unexhausted, procreating life-will'.[24] Altruism may be one expression of such a will, since it gives moral power over others, and my giving to you places you firmly in my debt. But there can be no such thing as utter self-renunciation – that too will be an attempt to gain spiritual superiority over others. And there is no reason why altruism should be the highest human goal. 'Life itself told me this secret: "Behold", it said, "I am that which must overcome itself again and again."'[25] So 'I have to be struggle and becoming and goal and conflict of goals ... whatever I create ... soon I have to oppose it ... thus will my will have it.'

The will is in a condition of perpetual struggle, conflict, and overcoming. What the will says is, 'I want to be – master over peoples ... the best shall rule, the best wants to rule.'[26] So the will 'needs steps and conflict ... battle and inequality and war for power'.[27] And now the dark side of Nietzsche makes its appearance, the side which was employed by the theorists of the German Third Reich to support their own perverse ideology. 'The word "good" was from the very first absolutely not necessarily connected with "unegoistic" actions', he says. It was connected with the idea of nobility, 'ultimately the good, clean, originally the blond-headed in antithesis to the dark, black-haired aboriginals'.[28]

The aristocrat, the 'good' is the 'man of discord, of dissension, the man of war', who says of himself and his peers, 'we noble, we good, we beautiful, we happy'. Such an aristocracy of power is what first forms the state – 'some herd of blond beasts of prey, a conqueror and master race'.[29] Perhaps Nietzsche is here only tracing the birth of the word 'good'. But it can easily seem, and indeed I think it is true, that he wants to carry this thinking over into the present, and show that the will to good is only a dis-guised form of the will to power, which is beyond ordinary notions of good and evil.

We who know how German National Socialism used the idea of a blond master race, setting out to conquer the world without being hampered by so-called moral principles, may shudder at where the idea of a will to power, unfettered by pity or

Was Nietzsche a Bad Thing?

compassion, led in the bloodiest half-century in recorded human history. It sounds liberating to be freed from 'tables of values' that have only expressed the *ressentiment* of the weak, and that glorify conformity, self-hatred, and life-denial. But if the price is perpetual warfare, lack of pity for the sufferings of others, and admiration for greed and ambition, we may wonder whether we should really admire he who 'laughs at all tragedies',[30] who calls us to 'live your life of obedience and war',[31] and who says that 'you should love peace as a means to new wars ... it is the good war that hallows every cause'.[32]

Perhaps we should applaud Nietzsche's exposure of much conventional morality as due to the resentment of the herd, as hypocritical and self-serving. Perhaps we should accept his celebration of human freedom, creativity, laughter and beauty, the Dionysian revelling in the things of the body and the earth, and his rejection of forms of Christianity that deny the body and the joy of earthly life. We should not want to be slaves of a tyrant God, and we should want to be creators who dance and joyfully affirm our earthly lives while they last. For it may seem that he is affirming humanity against the attempts of those who would suppress it by craven obedience to a peremptory and punitive 'tormented creator'.

But in the end does Nietzsche really affirm humanity? He despises most humans, 'the herd' – 'you will become smaller and smaller, you small people'.[33] We might resonate with his anti-Schopenhauerian sentiment: 'Life is a fountain of delight'[34] – but we might hesitate before the phrase that immediately follows – 'but where the rabble also drinks all wells are poisoned'. To regard most people as part of a rabble or herd does not seem very humane. And even of those who are not part of the rabble he says, 'I teach you the Superman. Man is something that should be overcome.'[35]

What is this Superman? 'A more manly, warlike age is coming ... live dangerously! Build your cities on the slopes of Vesuvius! Send your ships into uncharted seas! Live in conflict with your equals and with yourselves! Be robbers and ravagers as long as you cannot be rulers and owners.'[36] It is an age, apparently, of constant conflict and danger, where crime is common and where pity has been overcome, where the strong rule but are in continual danger of being overthrown. '"Man must grow better and more evil" – thus do I teach. The most evil is necessary for the Superman's best.'[37]

There is health and joy, exuberance and world-affirmation, but there is also egoism, struggle, conflict and war. In laughter and the affirmation of life, Nietzsche opposes the 'Spirit of Gravity, and all that he created'. This sounds attractive, until one reflects on what he created: 'compulsion, dogma, need and consequence and purpose and will and good and evil'.[38] We may wish to oppose compulsion, dogma, and need. But do we really want to oppose any form of purpose or good and evil? Even if the purpose is that we should be free, joyful and creative, and if that is the nature of true goodness? Deprived of all notions of objective goodness or moral constraint, Nietzsche's laughter sounds rather like the laughter of the pitiless warrior as he runs his enemy through, and Nietzsche's affirmation of life seems to be the self-affirmation of the victor in a bloody war.

In the coming age life becomes fully and openly what it always essentially has been: 'Life itself is essentially appropriation, injury, overpowering of the strange and weaker, suppression, severity, imposition of one's own forms, incorporation and at the least and mildest, exploitation.'[39] This is what life essentially is, and what the superman will be. It is 'man', with his moral scruples, timidity, and religious longings, who must be overcome. 'What is good? All that heightens the feeling of power, the will to power ... what is bad? All that proceeds from weakness.'[40] Humanity must be 'artistically refashioned' to allow the iron will, with all its inevitable risks and failures, to dominate.

The age of the Superman will, it seems, be an age of unlimited savagery, a war of each against all, where the common herd is despised, where no compassion is felt for weakness, and where there is no goal but the pursuit of power for its own sake. Nietzsche expresses the wish 'That you might grow weary of

Was Nietzsche a Bad Thing?

saying: "An action is good when it is unselfish."'[41] He declares that 'Courage destroys pity.'[42] The true prophet 'declares the Ego healthy and holy and selfishness glorious'.[43] So 'do not spare your neighbour! Man is something that must be overcome.'[44] 'Shatter, shatter the good and just.'[45]

Is this any longer humanism? 'Let us not be equal before the mob', he says.[46] Let us not be deluded by 'the retarding influence exercised by the democratic prejudice within the modern world'.[47] Perhaps to be beyond good and evil is to be beyond even the moral imperative to aim at the flourishing of all human beings, to promote their strivings for truth, beauty, and co-operative friendship. It must be so, for no moral imperatives remain for the Superman.

Has morality then been overcome? No, Nietzsche still speaks of 'good' and 'bad', though he transforms their meanings. There is a way in which one ought to live, and that way is based upon consciously discerning and realising the essential nature of life. Is this, after all, so very different from Schopenhauer's perception that compassion lies at the heart of reality, and when you discern that, you are committed to being compassionate? Is it so different from the Christian perception that active love and goodness lie at the heart of reality, and to realise that is at the same time to seek to be embraced by and to mediate that love more fully?

At this point it may begin to become clear that what philosophers believe to lie at the heart of reality seems to depend largely upon their own moral personality and perception. Kant saw a supremely rational and timeless reality hidden by the phenomenal world. Hegel saw a progressively self-realising Spirit expressed in human history. Schopenhauer saw an impersonal quiescent unitary ocean of calm beyond the frantic will-to-life of the human world. Nietzsche saw nothing beyond the will-to-power, seeking to blast away the last remnants of hypocritical social rules and religious repressions.

None of these views can count as dispassionate assessments of the nature of reality somehow inductively derived from common human experience. They are, in the great classical philosophers, more like literary creations (admittedly sometimes very boring and abstract ones – which is where Nietzsche can play a literary trump card) presenting personal perspectives on the nature of reality. It is because they are personal visions that we do not find or expect agreement between them.

Yet it would wholly devalue them if it was said that these perspectives are purely subjective – as though they were just optional and idiosyncratic stories that make no claim on truth. They all claim to give the truth, but to do so from a particular perspective, shaped by a particular culture and history. Nietzsche, for example, could only have written as he did after Kant and Schopenhauer, and in the Europe of the second half of the nineteenth century, when revolutionary social changes went hand-in-hand with new critical studies of the Bible and with the growth of Darwinian views of evolution.

Such perspectives carry a strong evaluative component. When Nietzsche says that 'The Christian faith is from the beginning a sacrifice: sacrifice of all freedom, all pride, all self-confidence of the spirit, at the same time enslavement and self-mockery, self-mutilation',[48] that is not a dispassionate assessment. He rejects God because he associates God with denial of life, of joy, of health, of beauty, of pride, and of courage. He must get rid of God in order to allow humans to be free. It does not really matter that the proofs of God have been undermined, or whether indeed they have (I have already argued that they have not been undermined, and that they are anyway misunderstood if taken to be quasi-deductive proofs). What matters is that God, as Nietzsche understands God, is morally objectionable and destructive of human freedom – a supremely ironic complaint from one who teaches that there is no morality against which to assess God, and that the exercise of supreme power is the highest of all aims, which a God would exhibit and therefore be worthy of our highest admiration.

Nietzsche has in fact replaced God by an even harder master, the will-to-power, a will to which we must be subservient (for we are not really free unless we are dominated by the will-to-power in us), which drives us to do things we may not desire (like living on the slopes of a volcano), which forbids some of the deepest human inclinations (like the inclination to altruism or to compassion), and which will finally overcome humanity itself.

The weakest part of Nietzsche's case is his assumption that human freedom is incompatible with the existence of objective moral standards, or with an objective will and purpose for human life. Why, after all, should freedom be valued? Is it just because we want to be able to do whatever we want, when nothing is objectively worthwhile, and when it looks as if our acts will in fact be determined in any case by the wants or desires we happen to have?

It is good not to be compelled against our will, no doubt – though in a Nietzschean war of all against all most of us will be so compelled and trampled upon by the victors. But then what? Always being able to fulfil all desires, whatever they are, is precisely the burden of the rich. It is often our society and social position that sets goals for action, which it takes self-discipline and determination to achieve. Such goals are set for us by our abilities, inclinations, by our training, education, and by our interactions with others.

It is in such contexts that freedom makes sense. Ideally, we are free to select and pursue such goals or not to do so. We select a goal because we think it is worthwhile. But we do not arbitrarily decide that it is worthwhile. Reflecting on our own abilities and preferences, and on the possibilities of our social situation, we may decide that a specific goal is attainable and appropriate, and we may decide to pursue it.

Goals and purposes are proposed to us, given by our personal and social natures, but we are ideally free to select and pursue one or more of them. They need not be imposed upon us, and to have a number of goals objectively presented to us is not a limitation of freedom. It is a condition of meaningful freedom.

So there may be a God who places goals of action before us – the pursuit of truth, beauty and friendship, for example. These will be objective goals and purposes. God may leave us free to select between them, and pursue them or not. That is a meaningful freedom, and arguably more meaningful than being told that you can do absolutely anything ('everything is permitted'), but there is no real reason to do one thing rather than another.

The irony is that Nietzsche does place an objective goal before us – the goal of generating the Superman, healthy, strong, pitiless, self-affirming, adventuring and all-conquering. That goal is disclosed by insight into the inner nature of the world, as expressing a will-to-power. But is that what the world is really like? Or are life, health, joy, freedom and creativity objective features of reality, whereas violence, repression and constant warfare are characteristics precisely of human wills that have chosen the competitive and individualistic will-to-power over commitment to the co-operative and universal moral goals that are inherent in the hidden depth of the world?

If there is a God who wills life, but who allows the freedom to choose it or not; who does not feel contempt for the common person, but offers forgiveness in place of condemnation; who does not offer endless repetition of life, but rather endless possibilities of growth in understanding, creativity, happiness and friendship; would this not be preferable to a philosophy that affirms suffering and evil as well as happiness and goodness?

Is there such a God? The reasons for affirming that there is are of the same sort, and are at least as strong, as Nietzsche's reasons for affirming that the secret of life is the will-to-power. It is possible to have an insight into the world as a realm in which goodness, beauty and truth exist as ideals to be followed, though self-will makes their pursuit difficult. Human experience may show traces of such ideals, in the intelligibility and beauty of nature, in the sense of human significance and dignity, in the inclination to do good even in face of adversity, and in feelings of transcendent depth and value that are so common yet so conceptually ill defined. These are forms of experience that lead to an affirmation of a deeper spiritual reality of supreme objective value beneath the appearances of the sensory world.

If Schopenhauer's sense of the tragedies occasioned by the

radically autonomous will, and Nietzsche's sense of the joy of life, are taken to be extreme responses to their insight into what it is to exist as a human being, then a mediating position might be that the egoistic will, bound to suffering and desire, needs to be overcome by a will that rests in something higher than itself, by a will to the Good and Beautiful. Plato still has something important to say, in a world that has seen some of the horrifying consequences that a negative interpretation of Nietzsche can lead to, and that has passed beyond Nietzsche.

Nietzsche declaims against restrictive and repressive interpretations of that spiritual reality. He offers in their place an affirmation of life and joy and creativity. But he is in danger of promoting irrationality, violence, conflict, egoism, and contempt for ordinary human beings, as ultimate human ideals. What his philosophy shows, in my view, is that if God is totally and consciously rejected, the reason upon which science relies, the values upon which human welfare depends, and the sense of human or personal dignity upon which moral sensitivity relies, are imperilled. That way madness lies.

There is good reason to preserve and strengthen the Western classical philosophical commitment to God, while recognising that the idea of God has needed and will always need to be rethought many times, and that it has sometimes been held hostage by negative and over-dogmatic forms of religious belief. There can be a view of God that affirms life, creativity, courage and joy. Perhaps only if there is such a God, such an ultimate reality, can these things be rationally affirmed in a world that is so often threatened by the chaos of violence and by the naked will to power. After all the intellectual struggles of the modern world, the God conclusion remains a real and living intellectual possibility, and perhaps a moral necessity, for all who are concerned to probe the deepest questions of human meaning and significance.

MATERIALISM AND ITS DISCONTENTS

I have been considering the work of some of the classical philosophers of the European tradition, from Plato to Nietzsche. I have shown how the great majority of these philosophers have expounded a basically spiritual view of reality. That is, they have held that ultimate reality has the nature of mind or consciousness, and that the material universe is the appearance or creation of that ultimate mind. Plato, Aristotle, Anselm, Aquinas, Descartes, Leibniz, Spinoza, Locke, Berkeley, Kant, Hegel, and many others all shared this general view. Even David Hume, a philosopher opposed to religious belief, who denied the existence of ultimate mind, did not suppose that matter could be ultimately real. Indeed, he thought that the material universe was a construct out of 'impressions' or 'ideas', and had no objective reality, or at least not a reality that could be rationally established. Schopenhauer and Nietzsche, who also rebelled against the God conclusion of most Western philosophy, still claimed that the ultimate nature of reality was not simply physical, but that it had a close kinship with specific sorts of human consciousness or willing (whether denial of will, in Schopenhauer, or affirmation of will, in Nietzsche).

Materialism has rarely seriously been on the agenda of classical philosophy. Democritus' theory that nothing finally exists except material particles with mass, position and velocity, interacting with one another in more and more complicated ways, did not have much appeal as a description of the value-laden, complex world of human experience, with all its depths of feeling and varieties of intellectual description.

I remember the occasion when materialism first hit the world of Oxford philosophy. In the early 1960s there were three main Professors of Philosophy in Oxford – Gilbert Ryle, A. J. Ayer, and R. M. Hare. Hare was an Anglican, Ryle an agnostic, and Ayer an atheist. But they all agreed that materialism was an over-dogmatic, impoverished and over-simplified form of belief that completely failed to account for the sheer diversity of the human world, the importance of human experience, and the exigencies of morality.

I was sitting in one of Gilbert Ryle's seminars in 1963 when a visiting Australian scholar, David Armstrong, presented a paper defending a materialist theory of mind. I still remember the sense of shock as this heretical Australian laid into Ryle's concept of mind and insisted on the need for a purely materialist account of consciousness. It seemed so far beyond the bounds of plausibility that some of us were not sure if it was tongue-in-cheek or not.

Well it was not. And in about forty years materialism, some-times called 'physicalism', has risen to a position of such pro-minence in philosophy that the materialist Daniel Dennett can say, quite falsely in fact, that virtually every serious philosopher is now a materialist.

It is easy to forget how very recent and meteoric the rise of materialism has been in philosophy. How could it get from being a joke to being a claimant to obvious truth in forty years? I think there have been two major factors at work. One is the rise of cynicism about any sort of idealistic approach to life, about all human institutions, including religious ones, and about the fail-ures of religious people to prevent violence and hatred, and indeed their tendency to increase violence and hatred in the world. This cynicism has been largely motivated by the Marxist 'hermeneutic of suspicion', the accusation that all religious and moral systems are in fact ideologies, no more than sophisticated disguises for egoistic self-seeking on the part of their proponents. Classical philosophy can thus be seen as a disguise for elitist social systems that privilege the sort of cultivated discussion that only leisure and wealth can bring. The realities of life lie further down, in work and physical effort. The material is the real, while the spiritual is a fictitious construct to delude the oppressed and keep them in their place.

When Karl Marx boasted that he had taken the philosophy of Hegel, and stood it on its head, so that the world is not the self-expression of Absolute Spirit, as in Hegel, but a purposeless and violent by-product of blind material forces, he described the dethronement of Spiritual reality exactly. The irony is that Capitalists as well as Marxists fell under this revolutionary spell. Capitalists may have resisted the idea of a centralised State-run economy, but they often fell completely for the idea that 'realism' requires that the profit-motive (the morally neutral capacity to satisfy any or all desires) is the real driving force of history, and that spiritual ideals are artificial stimulants to distract the attention of the toiling masses.

In addition to this sense that the material, not the spiritual, is the driving-force of history, the incredible progress of the natural sciences is the second major factor that has contributed to the rise of materialism. In medieval times the earth was a fairly small place within a larger spiritual universe. But at least it was at the centre of physical reality. Since 1600 we have increasingly come to realise that humans are a virtually peripheral part of a vast physical cosmos. Earth circles a star, which is one of a hundred billion stars in our galaxy, which is in turn one of a hundred billion galaxies in our observed universe, which is only one of who knows how many universes. The physical universe has expanded exponentially, and it has taken over the spiritual, so that instead of angels and demons we now have flying saucers and extra-terrestrials.

But it is not just a matter of size. Since 1953 we have become able to identify the mechanisms of human heredity, and possibly create our own successors in genetic laboratories. We have uncovered the structure of the brain, and can map just how it operates to produce perception and thought. We have built computers that may in future simulate exactly every human thought-process. It can look as if our increasing knowledge of physical processes is at last revealing the secrets of consciousness and thought. It is not only ideas that are ideological constructs. Now minds themselves are often seen as illusions produced by physical processes in the brain.

Classical philosophers began from what was most evident to them – their own experiences and thoughts. But now science seems to some to show that experiences are by-products of brain-processes, and brains can function very well whether or not conscious experiences exist. Thoughts are the dimly perceived epiphenomena of computational sequences in the brain-computer, which are the really effective causes of all our apparently mental behaviour. Marxism dethroned Spirit from having a primary role in how the world is. Science has dethroned consciousness from having a primary role in our understanding of the world. Thus materialism pricks the bubble of our spiritual illusions, and reveals that we are in fact computational, inefficiently designed and largely malfunctioning, physical entities without any larger purpose or meaning within the blind, pointless, freak accident of a wholly physical universe.

Some of the ablest contemporary philosophers are materialists. This is partly because it takes a huge amount of logical ingenuity to make the materialist programme seem plausible, so that it is an interesting challenge to good philosophers (just as the Christian doctrine of the Trinity was in medieval times, perhaps). But it should not be overlooked that philosophy is still a very diverse discipline.

Idealism, the view that mind or Spirit is the only ultimate reality, is far from dead, and many American University philosophy departments have a representative Process philosopher or Personalist – both variant forms of Idealism.

Phenomenology, the general view that analysis of existential, lived experience should be the basis of an analysis of reality, remains strong in European philosophy. Positivists also make experience primary, though they apparently have few feelings or existential crises, and prefer to have clear, distinct and unemotional experiences (which they call sense-data). Positivists have tended to think that their sense-observations are the basic data of rigorous science, and so they place a premium on sense-verification and the provision of sense-based evidence for all assertions. But Positivism actually undermines the possibility of public verification (since we cannot even verify that other minds exist), and it also undermines the claims of much modern physics that the ultimate structure of matter lies in unobservable but mathematically postulated entities.

Common-sense pragmatism, often in a Wittgensteinian guise, sceptical of all grand general statements about ultimate reality, and refusing to accept that philosophers are in any better position to say what reality is like than anyone else, is widespread. Such philosophers are fond of saying, 'Reality is in order as it is', without the help of philosophy. So their arguments are often devoted to proving that philosophical arguments in general are superfluous and misleading. The problem is that, when readers begin to believe them, they stop reading philosophy any more. This has regrettably caused a number of philosophy departments in Britain to close.

Scepticism, too, is far from dead, and resembles common-sense, except that it even doubts whether common-sense can be trusted. Some forms of post-modernism are sceptical views, insofar as they doubt whether there is any objective truth to be found. The main problem with scepticism is that its proponents tend to get very depressed, and often give up philosophy altogether, so there are not so many of them around.

Critical realism is quite popular. An intellectual descendent of John Locke, such realism maintains that perception and intellect do give us knowledge of objective reality, but show reality to be rather different from how things appear to the senses. Proponents disagree on just how different. For Locke a set of primary qualities – roughly, mass, position and velocity – are objectively real, while secondary qualities like smell, colour and taste are contributed by the mind. In modern physics those primary qualities have disappeared, and we have to talk of force-fields and wave-functions in curved multi-dimensional space-time. So sometimes critical realists are reduced to saying that there is definitely some objective reality which the mathematics of quantum theory describes. But exactly what it is we cannot be sure. It is what quantum theorist Bernard d'Espagnat calls a 'veiled reality',[1] since we cannot know exactly what concepts like 'imaginary time' or 'waves of probability' correspond to, if correspondence is even an appropriate term any more. As one critical realist has said, 'I cannot be sure just what objective reality is. But whatever it is, I most certainly believe in it.'

The dogmatism of materialism is very apparent when placed alongside these other more or less widely held philosophical theses. Materialists are metaphysicians in the grand manner. They claim to know what reality is, and that their description of it is, they think, obvious, accurate and rationally undeniable. Since that claim is doubted by most of their colleagues, it can hardly be quite as obvious as they say.

If modern philosophy is the application of reason to the widest possible set of known data, in order to obtain an informed judgement about what sorts of things are real, what sorts of things can be known, and what ways of life are most appropriate to the facts, it seems that we have to begin with the admission that there are many possible philosophical views, and none of them is theoretically certain, or even overwhelmingly probable.

It does not follow that they are all equally plausible. But it does follow that reason alone cannot make final decisions between a fairly wide spectrum of possibilities, ranging from the supremacy of Spirit to the supremacy of matter. What reason can do remains important. It can clarify basic axioms and aim to make them consistent with one another, analyse the strength and validity of inferences from those axioms, lay out a range of competing alternative axioms, test the consistency of an axiomatic system against the best available knowledge, and assess the strong and weak points of the general interpretation of the world that a rational system aims to provide. A rational philosophy is one that scores well on these criteria. But no philosophical view comes out as a clear winner.

It may be thought that at least some views – perhaps that of

Plato or Descartes or Bishop Berkeley – have been decisively refuted in the course of the history of philosophy. But I have sought to rescue all three from their critics, and show that their views can be reformulated in entirely plausible ways. Of course reformulation is necessary. The Theory of Forms, for instance, needs to be re-stated as a theory of objective mathematical axioms, and related more closely to experimental observation. But it then survives very well in some versions of modern quantum theory, and mathematicians like Roger Penrose can describe themselves as Platonists without embarrassment.[2]

It is not to be expected, then, that materialism is susceptible to a knock-down refutation. There will always be a possible reformulation of the view that mental phenomena are by-products of non-purposive and unconscious physical processes, and that our common-sense beliefs about the world do not represent the true nature of objective reality.

Nevertheless, materialism faces some very grave problems, largely raised by quantum physics. This is particularly annoying for materialists, since science tends to be a major plank on which materialism is based. The gravest objection is that it has become increasingly hard to say just what 'matter' is. If your philosophical theory is that everything that exists is composed of matter, it is frustrating to admit that you do not know what matter is.

For good old-fashioned materialists, everything that exists, or the one and only stuff out of which everything is made, is matter – solid particles located in three-dimensional space, with definite masses and velocities. When, around 1911, Rutherford bombarded atoms with alpha particles, the indivisibility and solidity of the atom was shattered. In 1924, de Broglie (pronounced 'de Broy') argued that sub-atomic particles could be treated as waves. In 1925 the first formalism for quantum theory was produced. From that point on, matter itself was subsumed under the wider concept of 'energy', which could take many forms. Electrons, from being tiny precisely locatable particles, were seen as prob-ability-waves in Hilbert space, only collapsing into particles under specific conditions of measurement. Even then, only the

Materialism and Its Discontents

probability of finding them at a specific location could be predicted, and Heisenberg proved that such waves/particles could not be assigned both a determinate position and momentum at the same time.

In modern quantum cosmology, virtual particles of indefinitely many different sorts flash in and out of existence in accordance with quantum laws, from a vacuum (lowest-energy) state of precisely balanced, but fluctuating, energies. Time and space are only four of ten or eleven dimensions that emerge from such a vacuum state, and there may be many space-time universes (of which ours is only one) that fluctuate in and out of existence from a more primal quantum foam, far beyond the forms of space-time with which we are familiar in experience.

Things have proceeded so far in quantum cosmology that physicists like Chris Isham, of Imperial College, and Stephen Hawking, of Cambridge, tend to say that 'imaginary time' is more real than real time, that the human belief that time passes (or that we pass through time) is an illusion of consciousness, and that human consciousness of three-dimensional space is a narrow subjective selection out of a multi-dimensional reality that we are unable to perceive.

Whatever all this means, it has left old-fashioned classical materialism far behind. The ultimate reality is beyond space-time as we know it, has a deep and complex mathematical structure, and is nothing like the world we see and touch and feel. It is certainly not made of matter, in the sense of solid bits of stuff, precisely located in three-dimensional space. Questions like, 'Where are the fundamental laws of nature located?', or 'How much time do quantum fluctuations in a vacuum take?' will be met with pitying looks by mathematical physicists. They (the laws and fluctuations, not the physicists) are not anywhere in our space, or at any point in what we ordinarily think of as time.

This means that the simple-minded materialism that insists that everything that exists must be somewhere, or that everything that exists must exist at some time, is just woefully ignorant of modern physics. There are supra-spatial and supra-temporal realities, realities beyond any and all spaces and times, and mathematical physics talks about them with an immense degree of sophistication and precision.

In the light of these considerations, it may seem that 'matter' is just a sort of thin and abstract skeleton, a desiccated substructure, of the richly observed world of human perceptions. This is roughly what Niels Bohr, one of the great founding fathers of quantum theory, thought. Bishop Berkeley was not so far wrong when he claimed that Locke's 'primary qualities' were in fact no more objectively real than the 'secondary qualities' that were admitted to be mental constructs, or appearances to human forms of sensibility. Primary qualities are a sort of abstracted and idealised mathematical ground-plan of the rich sensory world of experience.

As mathematical physicist John Polkinghorne has put it, 'We have no compelling grounds for regarding current theories as being more than a form of approximation to actual physical reality as it is encountered in the limit of effective isolatability.'[3] That is to say, mathematical physics deals with phenomena in artificially isolated experimental conditions, and even then provides only an approximation (though a remarkably precise one, within its terms of reference) to the 'actual physical reality'.

Professor Polkinghorne, as a critical realist, is convinced that there is an actual physical reality, modelled accurately, if not exhaustively, by our mathematics. Probably few physicists would wish to deny that. Put in another way, there was a real physical world in existence long before any human consciousness came into being, and somehow human consciousness emerged from it. But quantum physics seems to show that all that we really know of that world is how it appears to human consciousness, whether in perception or in mathematics or in some combination of both. We apprehend what our human faculties of sense and mathematical creativity allow us to apprehend. And we have strong reason to think that things as they are in themselves do not correspond neatly to things as we apprehend them.

Modern physics thus suggests a good deal of agnosticism about the hidden nature of the physical cosmos. It completely overturns the view of nature as a mechanical, deterministic and atomistic system – the 'clockwork universe' – and replaces it with a much more organic or holistic picture of an entangled, emergent, open, intelligible and semiotic universe. The quantum universe is entangled, in that non-locality – the correlated behaviour of widely separated ('non-local') wave-particles – means that no physical event is truly 'atomistic' – isolatable from the rest of the universe. Niels Bohr spoke of the 'inseparable quantum inter-connectedness of the whole universe'.

The universe is holistic, in that the nature of the whole helps to determine the behaviour of the parts. Larger systems constrain the behaviour of their constituent elements, and there are forms of 'top-down' causation that introduce causal influences that are not simply the result of the addition of many isolated causal factors. The whole is more than the sum of its parts.

The universe is open, because the principle of indeterminacy rules out the possibility of precise prediction of the future. It establishes probability as more fundamental than definite deter-minism, and sees the future as open to many creative possibilities, rather than as predestined to run along unavoidable tram-lines.

The universe is emergent, in that it develops new properties – like conscious awareness or intentional action – that are not wholly explicable in terms of prior physical states, though such properties seem to develop in natural ways from previous phy-sical states. For instance, subjective perceptions of the environ-ment and reasoned responses to it have developed by small incremental steps from pre-conscious stimulus–response mechanisms in simpler organisms. The evolutionary process seems to have an inbuilt propensity to form more complex, integrated and sensitive wholes, a sort of directionality towards greater responsiveness and creativity.

The universe is intelligible and mathematically beautiful to a degree that could not have been envisaged even a hundred years ago. As Eugene Wigner has said, it is an unexpected gift that the mathematical structure of the universe should be as elegant and rationally comprehensible as it is.[4]

Finally, the universe is semiotic, in that it does not simply re arrange its basic elements in different combinations. Many of those combinations are semiotic – they carry information. DNA molecules, for example, carry the codes for arranging proteins to build organic bodies. And perhaps the basic laws of the universe are computational, coding instructions for assembling new structures. As Paul Davies and John Gribbin put it, 'In place of clod-like particles of matter in a lumbering Newtonian machine we have an interlocking network of information exchange – a holistic, indeterministic and open system – vibrant with potentialities and bestowed with infinite richness.'[5]

If this is materialism, it is materialism in a new key. The physical basis of the universe seems to have an inner propensity towards information-processing and retrieval, that is, towards intelligent consciousness. The search for specific final causes or purposes proved a dead-end in physics. It was much more fruitful to seek precise mathematical descriptions of closely observed regular behaviour patterns. But in the twentieth century a more cosmic sort of finality re-emerged. The fundamental laws of nature seemed remarkably ordered towards the emergence of consciousness and rational control of the environment. To put it bluntly, matter seems to have an inner orientation towards the emergence of mind.

It is hard to conceive of such finality unless the goal of information and control is somehow already potential in the origin of the cosmic system. It is not surprising, then, that some quantum physicists think that something mind-like or conscious must lie at the very basis of physical reality. Eugene Wigner said that 'study of the external world leads to the conclusion that the content of consciousness is an ultimate reality',[6] and Von Neumann wrote that 'all real things are contents of consciousness'. For them, the collapse of the possibilities described by wave-functions into actual existents is brought about by consciousness. Their view may be a minority one, but it demonstrates the fact that quantum physics has moved so far beyond classical materialism that it is no longer clear that 'matter' is radically different from 'mind'. It could be that matter is just one form the objects of consciousness take, and that consciousness is needed to give definite actuality to its objects.

It certainly seems to be the case that the existence of consciousness and purpose in human minds is an unresolved problem for philosophical materialism, since there seems little prospect of giving a complete explanation of conscious experience in purely physical terms. If we have a view of the universe as intrinsically oriented towards consciousness, it is almost inevitable that we should think of this orientation as consciously intended. In that case conscious intention, and therefore mind, will not merely be the goal of the cosmic process, but its originating cause. That would make mind a basic and foundational, rather than a peripheral and unexpected, element of ultimate reality. And if there is just one independent and complete mind, not composed of separable parts, which generates all physical realities in order to bring into being sets of dependent and developing finite minds, that would provide an economical and elegant explanation for the existence of a physical universe.

But this hypothesis begins to touch the raw nerve and the emotional powerhouse of materialism. What really drives much materialist philosophy is rage at the injustice and indifference of the universe. Things happen to people by chance; the innocent suffer and the evil flourish. There is too much suffering and pain in the universe for it to be designed by any half-way benevolent being. Better, then, to postulate unconscious laws operating without benevolent purpose, than to think of there being a great intelligence that has intentionally planned such pain and pointlessness.

These are entirely serious points. If the universe is morally unjust and indifferent to suffering, that counts strongly against the existence of a just and compassionate God. But perhaps part of the trouble is that we think of a cosmic mind as able and wanting to avoid all suffering, and as immediately and directly rewarding the good and punishing the wicked. For a moment, set such an overtly religious but basically naïve picture to one side, and think just of a consciousness that conceives all possibilities and generates a universe directed to evolving other intelligent information-processing intelligences.

In a universe generated in such a way, chance and necessity, the conditions of open creativity and intelligible structure respectively, may be bound together in a complex way. Perhaps the general structure of the universe has to be the way it is, because the forms of its being are necessarily laid down in the basic mathematical array of possible worlds. And the selection of actual universes may be determined by goals that are worthwhile but hard to achieve and unavoidably susceptible to failure.

Plato and Aristotle struggled with this problem at the beginning of the European philosophical tradition. Their proposal (or one of them) was that the cosmic mind does not create matter, but shapes it to imitate and participate in the divine perfection as far as such a thing is possible. The material realm is one in which chance and necessity combine to form a structure with definite limits but also with possibilities for a certain amount of free creativity. The divine mind shapes the material in accordance with the intrinsic values of beauty and perfection that are inherent in its own being. But even the divine mind cannot annul the elements of chance and necessity that are inseparable from any material universe.

What seems to be cosmic injustice or indifference to suffering may be in fact an unavoidable consequence of the interplay of chance and necessity, inseparable from any material world, influenced but not wholly determined by the attraction of a divine mind that seeks to draw all things towards itself.

In general, this philosophical approach does provide a robust theoretical response to the reproach that good and bad fortune are wholly accidental, or that no alleged cosmic consciousness could seriously intend to create a universe containing so much suffering. A universe in which free creativity and genuine personal relationships are important has to be a world in which chance (undirectedness by some determining force) has to play a part – though chance always works within the limits of a more general determinate structure.

And the primordial creative mind does not intend to create suffering. Suffering is a possibility that cannot be eliminated from the necessary set of possibilities in the divine mind. Some suffering is unavoidably necessary in any universe that generates personally created values by beings that are an integral part of a developing, creative, dynamic and interconnected physical system. And much suffering is intensified in kind and degree by the self-centred choices of finite, free intelligences.

Philosophy cannot take us much further than this. But it may suggest that if there is a cosmic mind that is inherently perfect, yet has knowledge of every actual event, knowledge of suffering will be transmuted in the divine mind by its conscious inclusion within a wider and deeper experience. Since the divine mind has infinite time at its disposal, and intends the existence of distinctive values, there is some reason to hope that evil can eventually be overcome and eliminated, and might even be used to generate distinctive sorts of values – so that, while evil can never be justified by its consequences, all evil may nevertheless be turned to some otherwise non-existent good.

Finally, it seems possible that the divine mind could enable finite intelligences to share in this divine experience of 'redeemed' evil. If that could be, materialist objections to the pointlessness and injustice of life would be overcome by giving all sentient beings a share in a supremely valuable reality, to the precise nature of which they had made an important contribution.

To a materialist this will seem like a fantasy that just refuses to face the fact of death. Yet may it not be that it is the materialist who is refusing to see what is there? The clear facts of consciously valued experience and of freely chosen purpose, the intelligibility and elegance of the deep structure of the physical world, the visions of transcendent value in art, the categorical demands of duty and of the search for truth, and the testimony of so many to a felt power making for goodness and uniting the mind to a higher selfless reality of wisdom and bliss – all these things the materialist has to consign to illusion.

Materialism may possess the powerful attraction of economy and simplicity in its basic postulates, but it also has some major discontents. These are discontents that a materialist may feel, in trying to arrive at a wholly adequate and plausible account of reality as we know it in experience. They pose severe problems for materialism. And though the problems may be insoluble or may just have to be lived with, they remain sources of dissatisfaction for anyone who wants to adhere on philosophical grounds to a wholly materialist philosophy.

A first discontent is that the ultimate basis of matter now seems to be unknown. It is very unlike hard solid lumps of stuff. It seems to be a 'veiled reality', beyond space and time as we experience them. So it is not clear that consciousness, or some form of mentality or non-physical reality, possibly like a sort of mathematical or conceptual world, can be ruled out as impossible in principle. If that is so, materialism in the strict sense is no longer so appealing.

A second discontent is that consciousness – thoughts, feelings, sensations, images, and intentions – remains almost wholly inexplicable in purely physical terms. Materialists take out a blank cheque on the future, and say that we may find a physical explanation one day. But the truth is that no one has the slightest idea even of what such an explanation might be. The contents of consciousness seem to be new, emergent and irreducible sorts of reality, and even the most reductive physicalist occasionally feels a twinge of unease that there may be more to consciousness than matter.

A third discontent is that morality seems very difficult to account for in physical terms. Perhaps the human sense of moral obligation and the importance of pursuing moral ideals can be accounted for in terms of evolutionary psychology. But there remains a nagging feeling that moral values have a categorical and objective force that appeal to genetic or cultural imprinting alone cannot fully explain. To found morality simply on achievable compromises between conflicting human desires may be what the materialist has to do. But how then can we avoid losing that sense of self-sacrificial action for the sake of doing what is right and just, that most of us secretly admire?

A fourth discontent is that we would have to renounce any sense of an objective purpose in life. We might have to grit our teeth and bear it. We might even learn to enjoy the thought that we live in a pointless universe, where there is nothing for the sake of which our lives ought to be lived, unless we more or less arbitrarily decide on some ephemeral goal of our own choosing. Yet the sense that our lives, however obscurely, fulfil some sort of plan, or realise some 'proper' or authentically human possibilities, is hard to escape. Even Jean-Paul Sartre's determination to live in total freedom is, in some sense, a determination to live an authentic human life, to be what humans ought to be. We would really need to be very certain of the fact that there is no purpose or goal in human existence, to undermine the common human sense of purpose or destiny. The discontent is that we can never be certain enough of our theoretical disproof of purpose to be quite sure that the sense of purpose many people feel is illusory.

A fifth discontent is evoked by our commitment to rational thinking and to the postulate that our universe has an intelligible and rational structure. Philosophy, logic, mathematics and science all presuppose that it is possible and important to understand the world in a rational way, and that our theories and opinions are not just the products of complex chains of physical causes and effects which happen not to have been eliminated by excessive inefficiency. Commitment to reason points to the rationality of being itself. And whatever matter is, there is absolutely no reason why it should have a rational structure, or why rational thought should be able to discern that structure. The discontent is that materialism, in seeking to be the most rational way of understanding the world, seems to presuppose that there is a rational basis for the world, that the world is not just a chain of purely contingent physical causes and effects. Materialism always seems to be in danger of undermining its own claims by its undue concern for truth as an ultimate value.

A sixth discontent is that, for a materialist, there is no possibility of a final explanation of the universe. There is no possible explanation of why there is something rather than nothing, and of why what exists is the way it is. The materialist may reply that no such final explanation is possible on any view, and that we must all stop explanations at some more or less arbitrary point. But many, possibly most, philosophers have held that there can be a self-existent being, necessarily what it is and a source of supreme value. Humans may not be able to comprehend the nature of such a being in any adequate detail. But they can discern its possibility, and the fact that it must be a reality of supreme rational necessity and intrinsic value, from which the universe flows in an intelligible way. It is a major philosophical discontent of materialism that there is not even the possibility of such final explanation.

A seventh discontent is that the thoughts of some of the greatest philosophers and the experiences of thousands of the wisest and most morally heroic mystics and religious teachers, will have to be set aside as delusions. It is depressing in the extreme to view the lives and experiences of those who have loved the Good and the Beautiful for its own sake, who seem to have achieved the peak of human achievement and experience, and whose lives are transparently joyful, kind and gracious – and to conclude that they are founded on a mistake. I am inclined to say that, even if such lives are based on mistaken beliefs, it is better to live in such a way, and to do so would never give cause for regret. Where – as is actually the case – there is no objective way of deciding whether such beliefs are mistaken or not, it must be a cause for discontent that some of the most intense, reflective and creative experiences in human history will have to be discounted because of some rather abstract and highly disputed theory that only material things, and nothing but material things, exist.

These are some of the discontents of materialism. They do not demonstrate that materialism is false. But they may throw some doubt on claims to theoretical certainty that materialism is a true and adequate interpretation of human experience of reality, and of the nature of reality itself.

So I conclude with a question philosophy alone cannot answer, but with which it has wrestled throughout its history: Is consciousness an illusion, or is matter a myth? Is mind a late and transitory by-product of unconscious material processes that just happen to be what they are? Or is the idea of matter as a self-existent brute fact, without explanation or value, a purely hypothetical abstraction from our consciousness of a real, intelligible and value-filled world of experience?

What I have shown is that most European classical philosophers have inclined to some sort of idealist view. The consensus of the Western philosophical tradition is that there is a supreme and transcendent spiritual reality, though it can be conceived in a number of different ways. But human knowledge has expanded amazingly in the last hundred years. Has it brought the idealist tradition to an end? Or is it rather opening up new forms of idealism, still in the making?

In defending a series of what may seem to be presently unfashionable views in philosophy, I have made my own position fairly clear. I think the God conclusion stands firm, and that it is the best intellectual defence of the intelligibility of the cosmos, of the objective importance of our moral ideals, of an affirmation of the goodness, the joy and the beauty of life, and of the authenticity of those intimations of transcendence that provide some of the most sublime and transformative human experiences. But although I naturally believe that I am right, I entirely accept that the important thing is that we should go on asking the questions. It is, as Plato said, the process of enquiry itself that brings wisdom to the human mind. It is in that spirit that this small set of footnotes to Plato has been compiled.

NOTES

Chapter 1: WHY PLATO WAS NOT A WORLD-HATING TOTALITARIAN

1. Karl Popper, *The Open Society and Its Enemies* (Princeton University Press, 1971).
2. Plato, *The Republic*, trans. Francis Cornford (Oxford, Clarendon Press, 1941), ch. 31 (555B–562A).
3. Ibid., p. 312 (IX.592).
4. Plato, *The Laws*, trans. Trevor Saunders (Penguin, 1970), p. 447 (Book Ten, 910).
5. Plato, *Protagoras and Meno*, trans. W. K. C. Guthrie (Penguin, 1956), p. 157 (100B).
6. Plato, *The Symposium*, trans. Walter Hamilton (Penguin, 1951), pp. 93, 95 (211a–212c).
7. Plato, *Timaeus*, trans. Desmond Lee (Penguin, 1965), p. 40 (28).
8. Ibid., p. 45 (34).
9. Plotinus, *The Enneads*, trans. Stephen MacKenna (Penguin, 1991), p. 549 (VI, 9), trans. there as 'the passing of solitary to solitary'.

Chapter 2: WHY AQUINAS' 'FIVE WAYS' ARE NOT SO BAD AFTER ALL

1. Aristotle, *Metaphysics*, in *The Philosophy of Aristotle*, trans. J. L. Creed, ed. Renford Bambrough (New York, Mentor Books, 1963), pp. 126–8 (Book 12, 7).
2. Thomas Aquinas, *Summa Theologiae*, trans. Timothy McDermott (Blackfriars, 1964), 1a, question 2, article 3, pp. 13–17.
3. Richard Dawkins, *The God Delusion* (Bantam Press, 2006), p. 77.
4. Steven Weinberg, *Dreams of a Final Theory* (London, Vintage, 1993), p. 191.
5. Aquinas, *Summa Theologiae*, op. cit., question 5, article 1, p. 63.
6. Albert Einstein, contribution to Festchrift for Aunel Stadola, Zurich, 1929.
7. Dawkins, *The God Delusion*, op. cit., p. 150.

Chapter 3: Why Does Everybody Hate Cartesian Dualism?

1. Daniel Dennett, *Consciousness Explained* (Penguin, 1991), p. 37.
2. René Descartes, *Meditations on First Philosophy* (1642), in *Descartes: Philosophical Writings*, trans. Anscombe and Geach (Nelson, 1954), Sixth Meditation, p. 117.
3. *Descartes: Philosophical Writings*, op. cit., p. 281, from his Correspondence, no. 310.
4. Benedict de Spinoza, *Ethics*, trans. James Gutman (New York, Hafner, 1949), p. 274 (Part Five, Proposition 35).
5. Ibid. (Part Five, Proposition 26).
6. *Descartes: Philosophical Writings*, op. cit., p. 4, from a notebook begun in 1619 and copied out by Leibniz.
7. Gottfried Leibniz, *Monadology* (1714), trans. Mary Morris, in *Philosophical Writings*, ed. G. H. R. Parkinson (J. M. Dent, 1973), p. 192 (Proposition 81).
8. Leibniz, *Monadology*, op. cit., p. 188 (Proposition 58).

Chapter 4: Why Kicking Stones Cannot Refute Bishop Berkeley

1. George Berkeley, *A Treatise Concerning the Principles of Human Knowledge* (1709), ed. Mary Calkins (Scribner, 1929), p. 127 (First Part, para. 3).

Chapter 5: Why David Hume Is Odder than You Think

1. David Hume, *An Inquiry Concerning Human Understanding* (1748), ed. Charles Hendel (Bobbs-Merrill, 1955), p. 21 (Section 1).
2. Ibid., p. 58 (Section 5).
3. Ibid., p. 194 (taken from the appendix entitled 'An Abstract of a Treatise on Human Nature').
4. John Locke, *An Essay Concerning Human Understanding* (1690), ed. A. D. Woozley (Collins, 1964), p. 320 (Book 4, Chapter 1, Paragraph 1).
5. Hume, *Inquiry*, op. cit., p. 47 (Section 4, Part 2).
6. Stephen Hawking, *A Brief History of Time* (New York, Bantam, 1998), p. 141.

Chapter 6: David Hume's Un-Natural Theology

1. David Hume, *Dialogues Concerning Natural Religion* (1779), ed. Henry Aiken (New York, Hafner, 1948), p. 6 (Part One).
2. Ibid., p. 58 (Part Nine).
3. Hume, *An Inquiry Concerning Human Understanding* (1748), ed. Charles Hendel (Bobbs-Merrill, 1955), p. 45 (Section Four, Part One).

4. Richard Dawkins, *The God Delusion* (Bantam Press, 2006), pp. 113–14.

5. Hume, *Dialogues*, op. cit., p. 94 (Part Twelve).

6. Hume, *The Natural History of Religion* (1757), ed. J. C. A. Gaskin (Oxford University Press, 1993), p. 184 (Part Fifteen).

Chapter 7: How Kant Did Not Undermine All Possible Arguments for God

1. Immanuel Kant, *Critique of Pure Reason* (2nd edn, 1787), trans. Norman Kemp Smith (Macmillan, 1952), p. 276 ('Transcendental Dialectic'; 'The Ideal of Pure Reason', Section 3; B617).

2. Ibid., p. 316 ('Appendix to the Transcendental Dialectic', B726).

3. Ibid., p. 269 ('Dialectic', Book 2, Chapter 3, Section 1, B596).

4. Ibid., p. 239 ('Dialectic', Book 2, Chapter 2, Section 6, B519).

5. Ibid., p. 264 ('Antinomy of Pure Reason', B586).

6. Ibid., p. 267 ('Antinomy of Pure Reason', B591).

7. Ibid., p. 22 ('Preface to Second Edition', Bxxxi).

8. Ibid., p. 294 ('The Ideal of Pure Reason', Section Six, B653).

9. Ibid., p. 297 ('The Ideal of Pure Reason', Section Six, B657).

10. Ibid., p. 293 ('The Ideal of Pure Reason', Section Six, B652).

Chapter 8: Whatever Happened to Hegel?

1. See G. W. F. Hegel, *The Phenomenology of Spirit* (1807), trans. A.V. Miller (Oxford University Press, 1977), esp. the final two sections, on 'The Revealed Religion' and 'Absolute Knowing', which provide an admittedly dense outline of Hegel's thought on the issues discussed here.

2. The key work is: A. N. Whitehead, *Process and Reality*, ed. David Ray Griffin and Donald Sherburne (Macmillan, 1978; originally 1929), esp. the final chapter, 'God and the World'.

Chapter 9: Why Schopenhauer Was Not Quite an Atheist

1. Arthur Schopenhauer, *Manuscript Remains*, trans. Eric Payne (Oxford, Berghahn, 1988), vol. 2, p. 243.

2. Schopenhauer, *The World as Will and Representation* (1819), trans. Eric Payne (New York, Dover, 1969), vol. 2, p. 350.

3. Ibid., vol. 1, p. 62.

4. Ibid., vol. 1, p. 120.

5. Ibid., vol. 2, p. 583.

6. Ibid., vol. 2, p. 575.

7. Schopenhauer, *Manuscript Remains*, op. cit., vol. 1, p. 8.

8. Ibid., vol. 2, p. 198.

9. Ibid., vol. 2, p. 289.
10. Ibid., vol. 2, p. 628.
11. Ibid., vol. 1, p. 405.
12. Schopenhauer, *Parerga and Paralipomena*, trans. Eric Payne (Oxford, Berghahn, 1974), vol. 2, p. 325.
13. Schopenhauer, *Manuscript Remains*, op. cit., vol. 1, p. 81.
14. Ibid., vol. 1, p. 44.
15. Ibid., vol. 1, p. 35.
16. Schopenhauer, *The World as Will and Representation*, op. cit., vol. 2, p. 176.
17. Ibid., vol. 1, p. 412.
18. Ibid., vol. 1, p. 379.
19. Ibid., vol. 1, p. 411.
20. Schopenhauer, *Parerga and Paralipomena*, vol. 2, p. 201.
21. Schopenhauer, *On the Basis of Morality* (1841), trans. Eric Payne (Oxford, Berghahn, 1995), p. 48.
22. Schopenhauer, *The World as Will and Representation*, op. cit., vol. 1, p. 368.

Chapter 10: WAS NIETZSCHE A BAD THING?

1. Friedrich Nietzsche, *Human, All Too Human* (1878), p. 515, in *The Complete Works*, ed. Oscar Levy (New York, Russell and Russell, 1964).
2. Nietzsche, *Thus Spoke Zarathustra* (1883), trans. R. J. Hollingdale (Penguin, 1961), p. 186.
3. Nietzsche, *Twilight of the Idols* (1889), trans. R. J. Hollingdale (Penguin, 1969), 'The "Improvers" of Mankind'.
4. Ibid.
5. Nietzsche, *Human, All Too Human*, op. cit., p. 133.
6. Nietzsche, *Assorted Opinions and Maxims* (First Supplement to *Human, All Too Human*, 1879), p. 224, in *Complete Works*, op. cit.
7. Nietzsche, *Thus Spoke Zarathustra*, op. cit., p. 42.
8. Ibid., p. 58.
9. Ibid., p. 110.
10. Ibid., p. 61.
11. Ibid., p. 196.
12. Ibid., p. 199.
13. Ibid., p. 325.
14. Nietzsche, *The Wanderer and his Shadow* (Second Supplement to *Human, All Too Human*, 1880), p. 9, in *Complete Works*, op. cit.
15. Nietzsche, *Human, All Too Human*, op. cit., p. 39.
16. Nietzsche, *Assorted Opinions and Maxims*, op. cit., p. 33.
17. 'Why I am a Destiny', in *Ecce Homo* (1908), trans. Walter Kaufmann, in *Basic Writings of Nietzsche* (New York, Modern Library Giants, 1968), p. 9.
18. Nietzsche, *Daybreak* (1881), p. 9, in *Complete Works*, op. cit.
19. Nietzsche, *Thus Spoke Zarathustra*, op. cit., p. 161.

20. Ibid., p. 178.
21. Ibid., p. 331.
22. Ibid., p. 114.
23. 23.
    Beyond Good and Evil (1886), trans. Walter Kaufmann, in *Basic Writings*, op. cit., p. 260.
24. Nietzsche, *Thus Spoke Zarathustra*, op. cit., p. 137.
25. Ibid., p. 138.
26. Ibid., p. 227.
27. Ibid., p. 125.
28. Nietzsche, *On The Genealogy of Morals* (1887), trans. Walter Kaufmann and R. J. Hollingdale, in *Basic Writings*, op. cit., pp. 2–13.
29. Nietzsche, *On the Genealogy of Morals*, op. cit., p. 18.
30. Nietzsche, *Thus Spoke Zarathustra*, op. cit., p. 68.
31. Ibid., p. 75.
32. Ibid., p. 260.
33. Ibid., p. 191.
34. Ibid., p. 120.
35. Ibid., p. 41.
36. Nietzsche, *The Gay Science* (1882), trans. Walter Kaufmann (New York, Random House, 1974), p. 283.
37. Nietzsche, *Thus Spoke Zarathustra*, op. cit., p. 299.
38. Ibid., p. 215.
39. Nietzsche, *Beyond Good and Evil*, op. cit., p. 259.
40. Nietzsche, *The Anti-Christ* (1895), trans. R. J. Hollingdale (Penguin, 1969), p. 2.
41. Nietzsche, *Thus Spoke Zarathustra*, op. cit., p. 119.
42. Ibid., p. 177.
43. Ibid., p. 209.
44. Ibid., p. 216.
45. Ibid., p. 230.
46. Ibid., p. 297.
47. Nietzsche, *On the Genealogy of Morals*, op. cit., p. 2.
48. Nietzsche, *Beyond Good and Evil*, op. cit., p. 46.

Chapter 11: MATERIALISM AND ITS DISCONTENTS

1. Bernard d'Espagnat, *Reality and the Physicist*, trans. J. C. Whitehouse (Cambridge University Press, 1989), chs 10–11.
2. Cf. Roger Penrose, *Shadows of the Mind* (Oxford University Press, 1994), p. 412ff.
3. John Polkinghorne, *Exploring Reality* (SPCK, 2005), p. 34.
4. Eugene Wigner, 'The Unreasonable Effectiveness of Mathematics in Natural

Sciences', in *Communications in Pure and Applied Mathematics* 13, no. 1 (Feb. 1960).

5. Paul Davies and John Gribbin, *The Matter Myth* (Penguin, 1992), p. 302.

6. Eugene Wigner, 'Remarks on the Mind-Body Question', in *Quantum Theory and Measurement*, ed. J. A. Wheeler and W. H. Zurek (Princeton University Press, 1983), p. 181.